T0054871

Nazi Germany: A Very Short Introduction

VERY SHORT INTRODUCTIONS are for anyone wanting a stimulating and accessible way into a new subject. They are written by experts, and have been translated into more than 45 different languages.

The series began in 1995, and now covers a wide variety of topics in every discipline. The VSI library currently contains over 600 volumes—a Very Short Introduction to everything from Psychology and Philosophy of Science to American History and Relativity—and continues to grow in every subject area.

Very Short Introductions available now:

ABOLITIONISM Richard S. Newman
ACCOUNTING Christopher Nobes
ADAM SMITH Christopher J. Berry
ADOLESCENCE Peter K. Smith
ADVERTISING Winston Fletcher
AFRICAN AMERICAN RELIGION
    Eddie S. Glaude Jr
AFRICAN HISTORY John Parker and
    Richard Rathbone
AFRICAN POLITICS Ian Taylor
AFRICAN RELIGIONS
    Jacob K. Olupona
AGEING Nancy A. Pachana
AGNOSTICISM Robin Le Poidevin
AGRICULTURE Paul Brassley and
    Richard Soffe
ALEXANDER THE GREAT
    Hugh Bowden
ALGEBRA Peter M. Higgins
AMERICAN CULTURAL HISTORY
    Eric Avila
AMERICAN FOREIGN RELATIONS
    Andrew Preston
AMERICAN HISTORY Paul S. Boyer
AMERICAN IMMIGRATION
    David A. Gerber
AMERICAN LEGAL HISTORY
    G. Edward White
AMERICAN NAVAL HISTORY
    Craig L. Symonds
AMERICAN POLITICAL HISTORY
    Donald Critchlow
AMERICAN POLITICAL PARTIES
    AND ELECTIONS L. Sandy Maisel

AMERICAN POLITICS
    Richard M. Valelly
THE AMERICAN PRESIDENCY
    Charles O. Jones
THE AMERICAN REVOLUTION
    Robert J. Allison
AMERICAN SLAVERY
    Heather Andrea Williams
THE AMERICAN WEST
    Stephen Aron
AMERICAN WOMEN'S HISTORY
    Susan Ware
ANAESTHESIA Aidan O'Donnell
ANALYTIC PHILOSOPHY
    Michael Beaney
ANARCHISM Colin Ward
ANCIENT ASSYRIA Karen Radner
ANCIENT EGYPT Ian Shaw
ANCIENT EGYPTIAN ART AND
    ARCHITECTURE Christina Riggs
ANCIENT GREECE Paul Cartledge
THE ANCIENT NEAR EAST
    Amanda H. Podany
ANCIENT PHILOSOPHY Julia Annas
ANCIENT WARFARE
    Harry Sidebottom
ANGELS David Albert Jones
ANGLICANISM Mark Chapman
THE ANGLO-SAXON AGE John Blair
ANIMAL BEHAVIOUR
    Tristram D. Wyatt
THE ANIMAL KINGDOM
    Peter Holland
ANIMAL RIGHTS David DeGrazia

Available soon:

For more information visit our website

www.oup.com/vsi/

Jane Caplan

NAZI GERMANY

A Very Short Introduction

OXFORD
UNIVERSITY PRESS

OXFORD
UNIVERSITY PRESS

Great Clarendon Street, Oxford, OX2 6DP,
United Kingdom

Oxford University Press is a department of the University of Oxford.
It furthers the University's objective of excellence in research, scholarship,
and education by publishing worldwide. Oxford is a registered trade mark of
Oxford University Press in the UK and in certain other countries

First edition published in 2019

Impression: 3

Published in the United States of America by Oxford University Press
198 Madison Avenue, New York, NY 10016, United States of America

British Library Cataloguing in Publication Data
Data available

Library of Congress Control Number: 2019936265

ISBN 978-0-19-870695-3

Printed in Great Britain by
CPI Group (UK) Ltd, Coydon, CRO 4YY

For R. G. M.

Contents

Preface and acknowledgements

An Introduction is not the same as a concise history. It cannot just be a brisk catalogue of 'the facts' or a summary of the historical debates, and it must inform without oversimplifying. I have tried to meet this challenge by constructing a clear pathway through the history of National Socialism and Nazi Germany, but at the same time reserving some of my limited space for detours into selected examples of detail and interpretation. Taking my cue from the name attached to the republic that the Nazis overthrew, I use the city of Weimar, and the state and Gau of Thuringia of which it was the capital, to share the national narrative with the kind of regional urban and rural communities in which most Germans lived. And given how insolently the Nazis manipulated language as a tool of propaganda and prevarication, I also pause the narrative at times to probe some examples of the vocabulary used by and about them. Readers will be able to pursue their own particular interests in the rich body of literature suggested in the Further Reading.

A book without footnotes cannot acknowledge its sources in the usual way, but I have indicated in the Further Reading some of the most important texts on which I have drawn for particular topics. I am immensely grateful to Robert Moeller and Ulrike Weckel, who took time to read several drafts of the book. Thanks also to

Thomas Brodie, Patricia Clavin, Ruth Petrie, Nikolaus Wachsmann, and Oxford University Press's anonymous reviewers for valuable suggestions and corrections; and to Nicholas Stargardt for sharpening my ideas over the years. Special thanks to Susan Loppert for her steadfast support.

List of illustrations

List of maps

Abbreviations and glossary

alte Kämpfer	old fighters (term for the first 100,000 NSDAP members/ pre-1928 NSDAP members)
Anschluss	union (with Austria 1938)
artfremd	alien to the (racial) type
artverwandt	(racially) kindred
BDM	Bund Deutscher Mädel (League of German Maidens)
Blitzkrieg	lightning war
Blutfahne	(SA) blood flag
BRD	Bundesrepublik Deutschland (German Federal Republic)
CDU	Christlich Demokratische Union (Christian Democratic Union)
DAF	Deutsche Arbeitsfront (German Labour Front)
DAP	Deutsche Arbeiterpartei (German Workers' Party)
DDR	Deutsche Demokratische Republik (German Democratic Republic)
DNVP	Deutschnationale Volkspartei (German National People's Party)
Deutsche Gruss/Hitlergruss	German/Hitler greeting
Einsatzgruppe	SD task force

Endlösung der Judenfrage	'Final Solution of the Jewish Question'
erbkrank	hereditarily ill
Ermächtigungsgesetz	Enabling Act
Freikorps	Free Corps
Führer	Leader
Führerprinzip	leadership principle
Gau	region (territorial division of the NSDAP)
Gauleiter	regional leader of the NSDAP
gemeinschaftsfremd	alien to the community or asocial
Gestapo	Geheime Staatspolizei (Secret State Police)
Gleichschaltung	coordination
Heimat	homeland
HJ	Hitlerjugend (Hitler Youth)
Kaiserreich	German empire (1871–1918)
KdF	Kraft durch Freude (Strength through Joy)
KPD	Kommunistische Partei Deutschlands (Communist Party of Germany)
Kreisleiter	district leader of the NSDAP
Kristallnacht	'Night of the broken glass' (pogrom of 9/10 November 1938)
Land (pl. *Länder*)	state in German federal system
Lebensraum	living-space
Leistungsgemeinschaft	competitive or meritocratic community
Luftwaffe	German air force
Machtergreifung	seizure of power
Machtübernahme	takeover of power
Mischling	half-Jew (lit. 'half-breed')
nationale Erhebung	national rising
NSDAP	Nationalsozialistische Deutsche Arbeiterpartei (National Socialist German Workers' Party)
Parteigenosse	Nazi Party member

Persönlichkeitsprinzip	personality principle
POW	prisoner of war
RAF	Royal Air Force
Reichsstatthalter	state commissioner
Reichstag	national parliament
RM	Reichsmark
Roma and Sinti	German 'Gypsy' peoples
RSHA	Reichssicherheitshauptamt (Reich Security Main Office)
SA	Sturmabteilung (Stormtroopers)
SdA	Schönheit der Arbeit (Beauty of Labour)
Schutzhaft	protective custody
SD	Sicherheitsdienst (Security Service of the SS)
Sippenforschung	genealogical research
Sondergericht	special court
Sonderweg	special path (of German history)
SPD	Sozialdemokratische Partei Deutschlands (Social Democratic Party of Germany)
SS	Schutzstaffel (Protection Squadron)
SS-Totenkopfverbände	SS Death's Head Units
Stahlhelm	Steel Helmet veterans' league
Stand	estate
T-4	Tiergartenstrasse 4, HQ and code name for the 'euthanasia' project
Tracht	traditional dress
Volk	people or nation
Volksdeutsche	ethnic Germans
völkisch	ethnic
Volksgemeinschaft	people's or national or ethnic community
Volkssturm	'people's storm' brigades
Wehrmacht	(German) Armed Forces
Waffen-SS	Armed SS
WVHA	Wirtschafts-Verwaltungs-Hauptamt (SS Head Office for Business and Administration)

Chapter 1
Hitler myths

Hitler, the Nazi Party, the 'Third Reich': they overshadow the 20th century as a monument to all that is most horrifying in a century not short of other horrors. The disproportion between the scale of destruction that National Socialism brought to Germany and Europe and the brevity of its career is striking: thirteen years from the foundation of the Nazi Party in 1920 to the inception of the Third Reich in 1933, another twelve years until this regime went down in flames in 1945. At its apex stands the figure of Adolf Hitler, his features instantly recognizable from innumerable portraits, photographs, films, cartoons, and parodies, his gaze famously mesmerizing. But what will this face tell us?

Hitler's one-time economic adviser Otto Wagener voiced a common reaction when he recalled in 1946 that: 'From the first moment, his eyes caught and held me. They were clear and large, trained on me calmly and with self-assurance. His gaze came, not from the pupil, but from a much deeper source—I felt as if it came from the infinite.' Other contemporaries saw something repulsive: 'a jelly-like, slag-gray face, a moonface into which two melancholy jet-black eyes had been set like raisins'; 'mask-like, empty mouse-eyes, whose vaunted transfixing gaze turns out to be a mere dog's gaze from a pale, bloated visage'. George Orwell sensed something similar but, to his own disquiet, more appealing: 'It is a pathetic, dog-like face, the face of a man suffering under intolerable wrongs.'

Impossible to say today which of these interpretations is the 'true' one; they were as much the product of each observer's own convictions as of his vision. Hitler's first biographer Konrad Heiden once wrote that Hitler 'is never himself; he is at any minute a lie of himself; this is why every image is false'. Hitler is in a profound sense incommensurable, corresponding to nothing that we can now measure; he presents us with an intolerable task of bridging the gaps between the man, his image, and his crimes.

Writing in 1940, before the full magnitude of these crimes was inescapable, Orwell ventured to compare Hitler with the mythical Prometheus, the 'self-sacrificing hero'. This might seem a scandalous comparison, but it offers a clue to the relation between Hitler, his political movement, and the Nazi regime that this chapter will pursue. Its subject, 'Hitler myths', enables us to trace in bold outline the principal threads of enquiry to be explored in this history of Nazi Germany. A myth may be nothing more than a false or mistaken belief, and this is probably the most popular use of the word. But it can also be something more potent than this, a mode of communication which does not try to match the real world, precisely because the meaning of the world is not self-evident but needs to be deciphered and translated. A myth is required to exceed the rationally demonstrable truth, to magnify and supplement what is visible and tangible with a mystifying aura, but also to conserve an essential message. Each of the 'myths' that follows invites us to start thinking about the multiple, layered meanings that compose the history of Nazi Germany.

The survival myth

Late on the evening of 1 May 1945, German radio announced the death of Germany's Führer, Adolf Hitler, 'battling Bolshevism to his last breath'. According to the broadcast address by his designated successor Admiral Dönitz, Hitler had died 'a hero's death' in his headquarters in Berlin. He had fallen in defence of Germany, indeed of the civilized world, and Dönitz called on his fellow Germans to continue this historic struggle in the same spirit of dedication and self-sacrifice.

That was the official story. But we now know how much of it was true and how much deliberate falsification. Hitler had indeed died on 30 April, but not leading his troops into battle to save either Germany or the world. He died by his own hand, having induced his new bride, Eva Braun, to join him in suicide. To prevent identification, the bodies were incinerated and buried hastily in the grounds of Hitler's bunker beneath the Reich Chancellery, once the seat of Nazi power and now surrounded by Soviet troops. But at the time there could be no absolute certainty that Hitler was dead. Germans and Allies alike had ample reason to distrust declarations issued by the Nazi government, and in the confusion of those final days of bitter fighting in Berlin it was impossible to verify beyond doubt that Hitler really was dead. Even after Soviet soldiers reached the burial site a few days later and the charred corpses were discovered, their definitive identification was no easy matter.

For most Germans, the death of their Führer was by then less important than the daily struggle for survival on military and civilian fronts that had become increasingly indistinguishable. It was also less important than the hope that, with Hitler gone, a pathway to ending the war had finally been opened. As the news filtered through the embattled capital, a journalist noted Berliners' unemotional responses in her diary: '"So what? Finally! Unfortunately, too late.".. . People here are entirely indifferent whether their once idolized, beloved Führer is alive still or dead.' The relief felt by Germany's opponents was also tinged with doubt as Soviet spokesmen stoked uncertainty about Hitler's real fate, fearing Nazi plots to engineer a separate armistice with the western Allies at the last minute.

Yet whether born of fear, hope, or scepticism, rumours that Hitler was not dead began to circulate immediately. On 2 May, another Berlin diarist tormented herself with the impossibility of proof: 'Rumour. We feed ourselves on it... I sometimes have the feeling these days that nothing makes sense any more.' The rumours continued to proliferate after the end of the war, through the spring and summer of 1945, in Germany and beyond its borders. Hitler had escaped the Russians and was in British captivity. He had been wounded and was hiding in a monastery near Salzburg. His suicide had been committed by a trained stand-in. He had undergone plastic surgery and been smuggled out of Germany by air or submarine—Spain, Argentina, and the South Pole were favourite destinations. In July, the US State Department was said to be investigating a report that Hitler and Eva Braun had found refuge in Argentina, while a month later the *New York Times* reported that US east coast ports were searching incoming ships for Hitler. Long after any serious doubts ought to have been laid to rest, a US Gallup Poll in 1947 showed that almost half the American public still believed that Hitler wasn't dead. In May 1950, a West German magazine announced that he had fled to Tibet, while a poll by another German magazine two years later revealed widespread belief that he had successfully escaped abroad.

Stories of Hitler's survival were kept alive through the 1950s by the popular press across the globe. By the end of the decade, he had been sighted in virtually every country of the world except Russia. Israel's seizure of the long-sought SS official Adolf Eichmann in Argentina in 1960 sparked renewed rumours that Hitler, too, was among the many Nazis who had found sanctuary there. Intermittent allegations have continued to surface up to the present day in luridly opportunistic tabloid headlines ('100-year-old Nazi Dictator Found in Mountains of Chile!'; 'Osama Recruits Cloned Hitler!'; 'Hitler lived to 95 with his Brazilian lover')—all feeding the public appetite for a myth that, unlike its central character, has refused to die.

Yet there is more to the mystification of Hitler's death and the myth of his survival than public gullibility or commercial calculation alone. The myth of Hitler's survival was one of the fruits of his extraordinary powers of attraction and repulsion in his lifetime and beyond. For later generations, it has been impossible to let go of Hitler, whether as a metonym for a regime of unparalleled genocidal violence, an insoluble enigma of humanity's capacities, or, more disturbingly, as a figure of infatuating political potency. To suspend rational belief in Hitler's death, to invent plausible survival scenarios for the man and his regime, as so many novelists and scriptwriters have done since 1945, or to foster political dreams of a resurrection of the movement he led: these attitudes attest to Nazism's magnetic power, which seeps below our conscious defences of rational scepticism and engages some of our deepest fantasies. Even comic and parodic representations draw on this power of dread. Through his image of mythical enormity, Hitler has continued to shadow the darker reaches of our cultural imagination, testifying to the tenacious allure of 'what-if' visions of survival and return.

The totalitarian myth

The images of the massed faithful are familiar: rank upon rank of uniformed men, standing to ramrod attention, disciplined, biddable, threatening: not just the executive arm of dictatorship but its incarnation. And not only men, but women too: no less ordered, though perhaps smiling where the men are stern, the image of feminine submission against masculine rigidity; and children, the boys urging their slight bodies upwards towards manhood, the girls more decorous or restrained. This is the portrait of the nation under Hitler, readied for obedience: 'Führer befiehl, wir folgen Dir!'—Führer command us and we will follow you.

The Nuremberg Nazi Party rallies of the 1930s, with their carefully groomed audiences, have bequeathed us these haunting performances of the unity of Germany under its Führer: notably the 1934 rally immortalized by Leni Riefenstahl in her film *The Triumph of the Will*. It was there that Hitler's deputy Rudolf Hess, a man of doglike devotion to his leader, presented his receptive audience with a rhetorical encapsulation of the new Reich, his voice breaking with emotion: 'The Party is Hitler, but Hitler is Germany, as Germany is Hitler.' Playing on the conundrum of the Christian Trinity, this catechism offered a new mystery: the Führer, the Nazi Party, and the German people are one, and that One is Hitler.

This message was driven home in the innumerable speeches, slogans, and carefully choreographed iconographies that organized public opinion in Nazi Germany in the 1930s. Contemporaries and historians alike were compelled to try and make sense of this pervasive imagery, which repeated a novel political style already seen in Fascist Italy: the image of a nation not just mustered on parade, but somehow forged into a homogeneous mass, bound to its leader and his party by something more organic than mere loyalty. Italy had generated a new term for this antithesis of liberal democracy some ten years earlier. In 1923, opponents of the Fascist leader Benito Mussolini accused his new electoral law of abolishing parliamentary pluralism in favour of what they called a 'totalitarian system', a system that would enshrine the Fascist Party's immutable political monopoly. Not for the first time in history, a term originally intended as a criticism or insult was picked up and embraced by its target. 'Totalitarian' was soon adopted by Italian Fascism to represent its own aspirations to accomplish a 'total' transformation of society and the state, by means of a revolutionary ideology and politics that aimed to penetrate and renovate every sphere and aspect of life.

The Nazis themselves did not take to the term 'totalitarian'; as we will see, they pursued their own vision of the relationship between ideology, state, and society. But the word came to characterize contemporary political systems on the right and the left that not only disowned the principles and practices of pluralistic liberal democracy, but sought a total and violent transformation of human society, even human nature. There was no doubt that this was the objective of National Socialism: 'Genuine revolutions do not stop at anything', proclaimed Joseph Goebbels, the Nazi minister for public enlightenment and propaganda, in May 1933. 'There are no revolutions that reform or overthrow only the economic or the political or the cultural order. Revolutions are breakthroughs of a new *Weltanschauung* [world view]...At the end masses, *Volk*, state, and nation will have become one and the same.' Inevitably, 'total' transformation was a vain ambition, incapable of completion by any real measure. But, in the eyes of critics, there was a crucial element that totalitarian regimes seemed well on the way to achieving. This was the erasure of human aspirations to individuality and autonomy, and their incorporation in exactly the kind of quasi-organic mass, simultaneously mobilized and subservient, that was figured in the images from Nuremberg.

In the hands of a philosopher like Hannah Arendt, the critique of totalitarianism was a sophisticated meditation on the vulnerability of human freedom and the deformations of modernity. But following the defeat of Nazi Germany and in the polemical climate of the Cold War, western theorists of totalitarianism risked mistaking the control to which regimes aspired for what they actually achieved. These scholars intended to expose a generic contrast between the civilizing norms of their own liberal-democratic tradition and the outrage of the police state, whether Nazi or Soviet. So the image of the Nuremberg party rally exactly condensed this understanding of Nazi totalitarianism. It presented a technically perfect montage, managed and disseminated by an expert propaganda machine, that rehearsed the absolute power of the dictator over a nation of men and women, children and adults: giddy with self-abnegation, whipped into enthusiasm, manipulated by propaganda, cowed into submission, or effaced by terror. Total control, propaganda, discipline, intimidation: these were the building-blocks of the totalitarian myth.

'The Hitler myth'

A few months after Hitler's appointment as chancellor of Germany in January 1933, the French journalist Daniel Guérin commented on the behaviour of passers-by who had stopped to look at postcards of Hitler on display in shop windows:

> People who time and again have contemplated this banal, expressionless face, the dark wisp of hair, the bit of mustache, the well-waxed shoulder strap, still stop in front of the shop windows and defenselessly surrender to the hypnotic effect. There's an entire book to be written about 'the art of manufacturing a leader'...to see the Hitler myth slowly take shape and a vulgar human countenance attain divine majesty.

The capacity of this undistinguished physical being to dominate and manipulate by his oratory or his presence alone was legendary. But, as Guérin suspected, there was more to Hitler's potency than this, and the book he hoped for has since been written in the shape of an influential study by the British historian Ian Kershaw. Titled *The Hitler Myth: Image and Reality in the Third Reich*, Kershaw's dissection of 'the art of manufacturing a leader' not only pinpoints and proposes an explanation for Hitler's extraordinary popularity in Germany, but also suggests how the Third Reich functioned as a political system pivoting on his image.

The core of this Hitler myth is the proposition that a carefully cultivated image of Hitler endowed him with a mythical status and legitimizing power that exceeded both his own personality and the popular appeal of Nazi ideology (Figure 1). But this was not simply the effect of successful propaganda delivered from

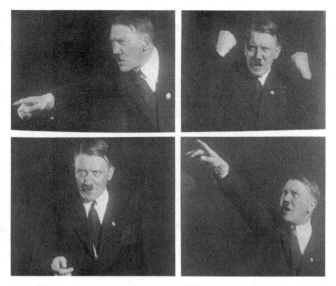

1. **Hitler the orator practises his poses before the camera of his official photographer Heinrich Hoffmann, in September 1930.**

above to a passively receptive audience. The essence of this myth lay in a more active mutual relationship between Hitler and the Germans, one that can be understood by invoking the notion of 'charisma'. For the German sociologist Max Weber, who incorporated this term in his typology of political legitimacy, charisma is not so much something possessed by a leader as a two-way communication between an exceptional leader and his followers: 'It is recognition on the part of those subject to authority which is decisive for the validity of charisma.' So with Hitler, it was what people attributed to him that was decisive; accordingly, the Hitler myth exploited ideas and attitudes that people already held, so that believing in the Führer appeared as an act not of ideological conversion but of recognition.

Guérin's window-shoppers were captivated precisely not by portraits of Germany's new chancellor, but by images of the Nazi

Führer. The word *Führer* itself is a commonplace noun in German; among its unremarkable meanings are not only 'leader' or 'head' but driver or guide, as in *Lokführer* (train driver) or *Bergführer* (mountain guide). And since all nouns are capitalized in the German language, *Führer* in principle carries no grammatically profound message for German-speakers. Even so, those living in Germany after 1933 knew the difference between *ein Führer* and *der Führer*. Hitler's courier and chauffeur Rochus Misch affirmed this when he recalled meeting Hitler for the first time in 1941: 'For me, he was, as he was for most other people, "der Führer"'.

The process of converting Hitler from one among many political leaders into *der Führer* had begun in the 1920s, almost as soon as the Nazi Party was founded. In the decade before Hitler came to power, Hitler and his closest followers fostered a cult of heroic leadership and superhuman personality which ratified his authority over the Nazi movement. When he was appointed as head of the German cabinet in January 1933, Hitler assumed the old-established constitutional office of Reich chancellor. But in mid-1934 this title was embellished with a new handle: Hitler's official title was now 'Führer und Reichskanzler'—in that order. After 1939, the remnant of the earlier political order was progressively discarded, and from June 1943 Hitler's official title, in all government and public affairs, was simply 'Der Führer'.

Crucially, the image of the Führer was manipulated to serve as the linchpin of a manufactured popular consensus that underwrote the legitimacy of the Nazi regime, despite its many sources of unpopularity, and that overrode its moments of danger and crisis. The Hitler myth, or perhaps better the 'Führer myth', insulated Hitler from rational criticism and the dangers of public alienation. Encapsulated in a tag that was popular at the time—'if only the Führer knew' (*wenn das der Führer wüsste*)—it enabled the ascription of unpopular or troubling policies and acts not to Hitler himself, but to the betrayal of his principles by self-serving henchmen in the Nazi Party, whether ambitious and corrupt national leaders or officious local functionaries. And this wilful myth of ignorance went on to function as a species of post-war alibi for many Germans. It salvaged an allegedly 'decent', defensible Nazism, and with this it sought to absolve the German people from responsibility for the catastrophes of aggressive war and genocide carried out in their name.

Otto Wagener, whom we met at the start of this chapter, was among those whose burden of belief was eased in this way. Wagener had served Hitler in several capacities before 1933 and had had hopes of a successful career in the new regime; but he fell from favour within a few months and retreated into private life. Yet his devotion to Hitler survived both his own and his country's disgrace, and after the war he sought absolution for his Führer by casting the blame for the shipwreck of Nazi Germany on Hitler's false friends. Wagener singled out Hermann Göring, Heinrich Himmler, and Joseph Goebbels as the 'three felons' who had 'assumed the terrible guilt of taking Adolf Hitler's thoughts and conversations as well as his actions and distorting or interpreting them quite unnaturally and covertly exploiting them for immoral and illegal, even criminal, actions'. So this Hitler myth, too, endured, once again outlasting the man and the regime.

There was more to Hitler than mythology, and more to Nazi Germany than Hitler. But, situated at different points between history and invention, between image and interpretation, between the wish and the real, these myths confront us with the key issues in the history of National Socialism: the nature of leadership and power in the Nazi movement and the Third Reich; the relationship between ideology, consent, and terror; and the dark stains of persecution, war, and genocide.

Chapter 2
National Socialism

The history of the Nazi Party before 1933 is dominated by two puzzles. How did it grow from its paltry beginnings on the fringes of the Bavarian radical right in 1920 to become the most potent political party in the Weimar Republic just over a decade later? And how did its leader, Adolf Hitler, come to be appointed chancellor of Germany on 30 January 1933? One short answer is that the Nazi Party was the beneficiary of two periods of exceptional economic and political crisis in the republic, in the early 1920s and the early 1930s. But for a full explanation, we need to step further back into the past, although historians have disagreed about just how far back we need to go and what we should be looking for.

At one time, it was tempting for historians to claim that the seeds of National Socialism had been sown in German history centuries earlier; or, more plausibly, that recent German history showed peculiarities—deformities, even—that diverted it from the normal path of industrialization, modernization, and democratization in western Europe and the USA, and set it on a fatal 'special path' (*Sonderweg*) culminating in National Socialism. Nowadays, there is broad consensus that there is no such thing as a 'normal' history from which Germany deviated, but only differing processes of historical change. There is much agreement, too, that we can better understand the sources of Nazism if we don't head too far back into Germany's distant past, but focus instead on the dynamics of its more recent history: the political culture of post-unification imperial Germany between 1890 and 1914, and the rupture brought by the First World War. We cannot grasp the magnitude of this rupture if we have not first encountered the society whose foundations it shook. This is the perspective I will adopt here, because it isolates one of the key determinants of the character of the Nazi movement and Nazi Germany: the history of how Germans engaged with the process of imagining, building, and sustaining nation and community.

What exactly 'Germany' was and who was a German remained an unresolved question during the mid-19th-century era of unification, which was brought to a provisional political closure with the merging of twenty-seven states into the German empire in 1871. Although the chancellor Otto von Bismarck had famously spoken in 1862 of the need for 'iron and blood'—war—to resolve the German national question, the tools of actually experienced nationhood are less blunt. How are nations made, not just militarily and politically but intellectually, culturally, emotionally? Who belongs and who does not—and who decides this?

The answers to these questions are complicated because they are partly cultural constructs, the products of ideology and desire as much as empirically demonstrable facts. They were the processes through which modern European states forged their variants of national identity and citizenship in the course of the 19th century. In Germany these questions remained on the agenda well after 1871, attracting different answers in its constituent states as well as from the major political camps—conservatives, liberals, Catholics, and socialists. We should remember that a history told from any of these other perspectives would look markedly different from the narrative of National Socialism that shapes this book. But what is important is that these questions were unresolved in 1914; they returned with a vengeance in 1918; they dominated the politics of National Socialism before 1933 and after the Nazis took power.

'National Socialism'

What we usually call the Nazi party was announced to the public, at its founding meeting in Munich in February 1920, as the 'Nationalsozialistische Deutsche Arbeiterpartei' (NSDAP), the National Socialist German Workers' Party. 'Nazi' is how the first syllables of this name are pronounced in German, but it was not what the members of the new party called themselves. That belittling abbreviation was bestowed by some of their first opponents in Bavaria; it was imported into English by German political émigrés in the 1930s and has remained the recognized shorthand. But it also blurs the origins and meaning of the party's full name and ideology. The members of the new party preferred to call themselves 'National Socialists', a title that embodied a historic aspiration carried over from late 19th-century Germany.

Imperial Germany has often been characterized as authoritarian and defensive, centred on an autocratic monarchy and self-interested elites who were unwilling to concede political power to emergent social groups. There is certainly truth in this, but Germany's pre-1914 political culture was far from paralysed, and from the point of view of the imperial regime's supporters its vitality and diversity were part of the problem. Despite significant restrictions on political freedom, the German parliament (Reichstag) was elected by universal male suffrage, and its liberal, Catholic, and social democratic opposition parties represented at least two-thirds of German voters on the eve of the war. With its million members and over four million voters, the SPD (Sozialdemokratische Partei Deutschlands) was the largest socialist party in Europe, and projected itself as a kind of alternative political universe, driving towards a new post-capitalist vision of socialism and internationalism.

While the German elites struggled to safeguard their political reach and power against the growing challenge of constitutionalist and socialist parties, nationalists began to mobilize independently of their patrician social superiors. They adopted a new political dynamism and proposed new political agendas, including an aggressively expanded notion of German *Lebensraum* (living-space) and a defensively narrow definition of German citizenship. Drawing on a widely recognized vocabulary of German identity and community, they aspired to override the semantics of class, social conflict, and international proletarian solidarity by invoking a culturally and ethnically homogeneous *Volk*—a national people or ethnic nation—as the precondition for Germany's stability and strength. Long before the Nazis marked it with their own stamp, 'National Socialism' was a slogan distilling the claim that the mutual antagonism of the era's two dominant political ideologies could be overcome by merging them into an explicitly German species of national ethnic community—a *Volksgemeinschaft*—under strong leadership. There were conservative and even liberal variants of this vision of social and political order. Bismarck, who had attempted to combine an authoritarian political system with an innovative social policy, was dubbed 'the first national socialist' by an aristocratic commentator in 1887. The liberal-nationalist Friedrich Naumann argued that his National Social party, founded in 1896, would demonstrate that 'Nationalism and socialism can be blended into a political unity that will be true to both'.

Radical ethnic nationalism was not necessarily more conspicuous in Germany than elsewhere. In its most extreme form it was confined to the political fringes, and it is largely hindsight that makes it seem so much noisier and more threatening there. Various combinations of muscular patriotism, political authoritarianism, and racially inflected nationalism could be found all over pre-1914 Europe as states negotiated their paths to nationhood. Yet it is arguable that the German notions of the *Volk* that underpinned the extremes of radical nationalism were invested with something more than just the standard affirmations of cultural unity and patriotic primacy that could be found everywhere else. Disseminated most explicitly as *völkisch* thought, these ideas conveyed notions of an organic *Volksgemeinschaft*, a racial community bound by shared blood, rooted in common clay, charged with the duty to expand or perish. As a correlate, *völkisch* groups also demanded the exclusion of those who did not fit into the community defined in these terms: minorities such as Poles or Jews, and potentially other kinds of 'outsiders' too. In this vein, they aspired to convert or marginalize the social democrats, whom they dismissed as *vaterlandslos*—internationalists 'without a fatherland'.

These fringe groups looked too for a new style of inspirational leadership and a purified political and cultural armoury that would equip Germany to resist the competition of other nations. They articulated the aspirations of men (more rarely women) impatient to secure their country against domestic and international threats, and frustrated by what they saw as the elites' failures to address this. On both sides of the watershed of 1918, these ideas appealed to some who feared that their interests were protected by neither capitalism nor social democracy. In the villages and small towns where most Germans still lived, familiar sources of individual identity and communal cohesion persisted, yet also seemed under threat from the pace of urban and industrial growth, despite its economic benefits. For others, life's frustrations and disappointments could be projected onto a larger screen of resentment and fantasy, populated not only by an uncaring political class but by anonymous, cosmopolitan puppet-masters of capitalism and urban mass society: financiers and speculators, industrial and commercial cartels, liberals, socialists, and Marxists, freemasons, and feminists, a whole spectrum of the less-than-fully-German.

Seeded through this cabal of alien forces were 'the Jews', depicted as a nomadic, unmanly, materialistic people that lacked the organic bonds of territory and the spiritual values of nationhood, and were instead parasitical on their host societies. In everyday political translation, *Judenhass* (Jew hatred) reduced to the argument that Judaism was quintessentially un-German, and that

16

Germans must defend themselves against the Jews' 'subversion' of their nation and their values. The term 'antisemitism' was coined by the German journalist Wilhelm Marr in the 1880s, but the prejudice itself was by no means peculiar to Germany. Throughout Europe it functioned more as a widely shared social code than as a consistent ideology or political programme; 'scientific' racial antisemitism was marginal, including in Germany. But cognate ideas and values—the national/ethnic people or *Volk*; the concept of community rather than society; anti-Marxism, anti-materialism, anti-feminism; an investment in strong leadership; and a mix of belligerent confidence and defensive unease—colonized the right wing of imperial Germany's political culture without fully defining it. This was the mental universe into which the first generation of Nazi leaders was born in the 1880s and 1890s, providing an ideological reservoir on which they were to draw after 1918.

Adolf Hitler

It is always risky to try to capture the mood of an age in this way, even more so to nominate an individual as its representative, but Adolf Hitler—Austrian by birth, German by vocation—surely fits this bill as well as anyone. Born in modestly respectable circumstances in 1889 in Braunau am Inn, a small Austrian town poised on the frontier with Germany, Hitler hankered after an artistic career, an ambition that drew him at the age of 18 to Vienna. The capital of the sprawling Austrian-Hungarian empire, *fin-de-siècle* Vienna was a febrile mosaic of cultural and political contradictions. It was a magnet for the immigration and assimilation of Jews—as well as Czechs, Poles, and all the other ethnic minorities of the multinational empire—but it was also a seat of Zionism. It was a stronghold of social democracy that was nevertheless governed by the antisemitic demagogue Karl Lueger and his Christian Social party. Its islands of artistic modernism and intellectual bohemianism were marooned in an ocean of aristocratic hauteur and bourgeois respectability.

Here for five years Hitler was confronted with the cosmopolitan cultural and ethnic kaleidoscope of big-city life at the same time as he faced the cruel frustration of his artistic aspirations. Twice rejected by the Academy of Fine Arts, he retreated into a world of self-pity, moody indolence, and self-indulgent fantasy, absorbing a politics of distrust from his drifting life. But his later depictions of Vienna as a time of trial, a revelation of the mortal peril posed by the Jewish race and of his own life's purpose, are unreliable. At this point his political interests were minimal; he seems to have been, if anything, a German nationalist with no love lost for Vienna's cosmopolitanism or for the internationalism of social democracy and the Catholic church. So little did he honour his native land that, in 1913, he dodged the Austrian draft and shifted himself to the more congenial environment of Munich, the capital of the Bavarian monarchy. There, on the outbreak of war, Hitler enlisted enthusiastically in the Bavarian army. Austria was left behind: Hitler was making himself into a German in Germany, the first step on a road to remaking Germany itself.

War and revolution

The historical significance for the future of Germany of the war that began in August 1914 can scarcely be exaggerated. It had a profound effect on Hitler, giving purpose to his nationalism and inculcating an intemperate rage against shirkers and defeatists. It also changed the rules of German politics—or rather, it was the war that ended in November 1918 in armistice and revolution that did this, splitting the country and amplifying the political ambitions and ideological belligerence of the radical right. The rigours of a conflict that we have since learned to treat as an existential tragedy were grasped at the time in radically different terms. A war that began by inflating the expectations of German nationalists ended by stoking their sense of betrayal. They came out of it having glimpsed the possibility that the war might have yielded all that it had initially promised: a new national solidarity, a glorious test of German manhood, victory, continental power, a vast empire in eastern Europe. But what it actually brought was calamity: over two million war dead and twice as many wounded or crippled; international humiliation; a devastated economy; social and political polarization, democratic revolution, and a virtual civil war.

In November 1918, Germany's dynasties were toppled and a republic was proclaimed, followed in August 1919 by the adoption of the new Weimar constitution and a fully democratic franchise: mighty achievements for liberals and democrats, but hammer blows to the nationalist right. Almost simultaneously came the crushing terms of the Treaty of Versailles, including confiscations of German territory, the decimation of its armed power and frontier defences, and the infamous 'war guilt clause', which enabled the Allies to impose heavy reparations (financial liabilities) on the pretext of Germany's sole responsibility for the war. For many Germans, this was bitter evidence that the long years of blood and sacrifice demanded by total war had been comprehensively betrayed.

There were few Germans who did not feel the injustice of Versailles keenly; yet most nevertheless bent themselves to remaking their lives and their country in this challenging post-war universe, many with creative energy and enthusiasm, others with more than a degree of resignation. But radical nationalists remained unreconciled to the legacy of the 'November criminals', their term for the democrats and socialists they held responsible for the republic and Versailles. For some soldiers, the war had not quite ended in 1918 anyway. Thousands, including many who later became leading Nazis as well as rank-and-file members of the NSDAP and its paramilitary squads the SA and the SS (Schutzstaffel/Protection Squadron), found their way into militias defending Germany against revolutionary Bolsheviks at home and Slav and Baltic nationalists on its 'bleeding frontiers' in the east. Although soldiers and militias alike eventually returned to ordinary civilian life, enough remained trapped in the wartime values of militarism and masculine comradeship to carry a cult of violence and sacrificial martyrdom deep into the political life of the new republic.

On top of this, the shocking outcome of the war was repeatedly attributed to a mendacious but attractive and politically fateful explanation. The widespread claim that the German army had not been defeated on the battlefield before the November armistice was elaborated into a myth that it had been 'stabbed in the back' by traitors on the home front. This duplicitous catchphrase was first recorded in a speech by the war hero and later president General Paul von Hindenburg in November 1919, but by then the military leadership had already long disowned their true responsibility for Germany's defeat. Hitler's own commanding officer assured his men in December 1918 that their regiment 'knows itself to be free from guilt about the disastrous outcome of the war'. The calamity seemed so profound that many on the radical right could grasp it only as the product of a deep-seated 'Jewish-Bolshevik' conspiracy against which the imperial elites had proved defenceless. In their eyes, the German national community had been cynically thrown away. The republic was a sham, its leaders traitors, its beneficiaries un-German. Fortified by this political mythology, *völkisch* and radical nationalist sentiment claimed a new political foothold, and looked for a new beginning.

Chapter 3

From Munich to Berlin (via Weimar)

The NSDAP was one product of the new political and social universe in post-war Germany and many of its neighbouring states: societies struggling to recover from war in newly democratic frameworks that carried great promise as well as risks. In Germany, the republic's diverse civic energies and creative cultural vitality, its wide range of ideologies and loyalties across the political spectrum must not be forgotten as we trace the history of the NSDAP, a party that was largely irrelevant to it until 1930. But what the republic would mean in practice was far from clear. Through the 1920s, it was not yet a secure democracy, but rather a system of republican pluralism supported by liberals and social democrats but repudiated by political and economic elites, the nationalist right and the communist left. The new state was a work in progress: a clear rejection of autocratic rule, but not yet a dependable blueprint for the future shape of citizenship, community, and identity. It left the relationship between capital and labour unresolved, and its compatibility with the left's social revolutionary ambitions was deeply divisive.

In Germany's socially divided cities, political engagement initially coexisted with sporadic armed struggle as the legitimacy of the republic was contested from both left and right. While the SPD leadership backed the republic, the newly founded Communist Party (KPD) fought for power in streets and workplaces as well as in elections—locking the two parties of the left into an unrelenting mutual antagonism. At the other end of the spectrum, *völkisch* and radical nationalists were energized by the nightmare of revolution and republic, by the perceived humiliation of Versailles and threat of Bolshevism following the Russian revolution. Those who did not find a political home in the patrician German nationalist party (DNVP) were drawn to more grassroots groupings whose lingua franca was an increasingly strident antisemitism and revanchism, reinforced by populist anti-Bolshevism and fantasies of national rebirth. Across the spectrum, uniformed paramilitary associations gathered defensively on the edges of party politics, testifying to the constitution's uncertain power to bridge the deep fault-lines of the post-war nation: the Nazis' SA, the communist Rotfrontkämpferbund (Red Front Fighters' League), the democratic-left Reichsbanner, and the nationalist Stahlhelm (Steel Helmet), part political movement and part veterans' troop.

Munich

Munich, the headquarters of the Nazi Party and the city to which Hitler returned at the end of the war, was among Germany's divided cities. A dynastic capital prized for its bourgeois elegance and bohemian tincture, Munich was also a rapidly growing industrial centre with a strong socialist movement. In 1918/19, the city saw fierce battles for the control of Germany's future, including a brief episode of far-left revolutionary rule which was followed by one of the bloodiest counter-revolutionary reactions in all of Germany. Munich then became the seat of a deeply conservative-nationalist Bavarian state government profoundly at odds with the republic, and seen by many across the political spectrum as a potential launching pad for a right-wing national coup.

The embryonic Nazi Party—the Deutsche Arbeiterpartei (DAP), established in February 1919—was one among Munich's panorama of small, unstable groups on the far reaches of the antisemitic right. Posted by army intelligence to inform on it, Hitler found a milieu in which to nurture his radical antisemitism and to expand his already impressive talents as a fiery orator and unprincipled opportunist. Since he was otherwise ill-equipped for life after the army, Hitler now conceived his future as a political agitator, with the DAP small enough for him to quickly make his mark. A year later, the rapidly growing party was relaunched as the NSDAP, and in July 1921 Hitler was able to hoist himself into its leadership.

The Nazi Party at this time was a mosaic of the different political dynamics driving the *völkisch*, radical nationalist, and antisemitic right. It was an organization of raucous propaganda and would-be popular mobilization, selling the image of a violated nation that could be made whole again; a disciplined sect increasingly devoted to a personal leader; a player in the back rooms of elite politics and patronage; and an engine of insurrection powered by the SA. These were the building-blocks of a new political style gathering pace simultaneously in Italy, where, to Hitler's fascination, Mussolini's Fascist Party stood on the verge of claiming power. But in Hitler's first years in the NSDAP, it was no more than a provincial fringe party; and Hitler—contrary to the heroic role he ascribed himself retrospectively—was more at the mercy of its internal dynamics than in control of them.

By 1923, the NSDAP was approaching 50,000 members (when Hitler had joined the DAP in 1919, he was number 55)—invisible in national terms, but impressive in Bavaria. Its membership came from all social groups, but more than half from the same lower-middle-class strata whose aspirations and anxieties had helped fuel the pre-war *völkisch* movements. Hitler's public speeches sharpened these sentiments and articulated their seductive political logic in the tense post-war conditions, in which fears stoked by the Russian Bolshevik revolution were widespread and talk of right-wing insurrection rife. With a mix of populist rhetoric and raw antisemitic invective, as well as a brazen disregard for veracity, Hitler proved to be a popular speaker, hammering home messages that his audiences wanted to hear. He claimed that no other party was willing to trust the people or mobilize their energies for the mammoth tasks confronting Germany: not just recovery from defeat and domestic division, and liberation from foreign domination, but the salvation of an organic German community from the existential threat of Judaism and Bolshevism.

For a conspiratorial antisemitic mindset, it was perfectly plausible to see 'the Jews' as insidious agitators for international proletarian revolution on the Russian model, yet at the same time as predatory capitalists, war profiteers, and foreign bankers sucking reparations out of a prostrate Germany. Antisemites saw these as twin forces in a racial pincer movement dedicated to the exploitation, subversion, and eventual extinction of the German people. In this 'gigantic struggle', Hitler argued in an April 1922 speech, 'there are only two possibilities...either the victory of the Aryan side, or its annihilation and victory for the Jews'. This dichotomous message shifted politics from the realm of the practical to the utopian, from the ground of political calculation and compromise to that of existential risk. It was ground Hitler was to inhabit for the rest of his life: the stakes were so high that any gamble was justifiable.

The balance between the impulses at play in the Nazi movement spiralled out of control in the chaotic year of 1923, when the republic was convulsed by France's invasion of the Ruhr industrial region, in response to the non-payment of a tranche of reparations. A shakily recovering German economy was forced into reverse and inflation spiralled dizzily out of control. The value of money was destroyed (in November 1923, one US dollar was worth 4.2 trillion Reichsmark); the normal world was turned upside down, and the government struggled to control the ensuing political turmoil. In the midst of these crises, on 9 November 1923, Hitler, driven by his high-stakes rhetoric and increasingly reliant on the unruly SA, launched an armed assault on government offices in Munich. Hitler believed that his 2,000-strong militia would be raising the banner for the takeover of national government in

Berlin by his patrons, the Bavarian politicians and army officers who had been playing with the idea of a national coup. But their support fizzled when the German army refused its backing. Hitler's putsch was an abject failure, yet it was converted in Nazi mythology into a testimony of heroic martyrdom, the first act in the coming 'national uprising' (*nationale Erhebung*).

Hitler was arrested, tried, and imprisoned (though a sympathetic judge and influential friends saw to it that his sentence was both brief and mild). The NSDAP was banned throughout Germany, and the *völkisch* movement dissolved into cantankerous warring factions. Hitler sat out his prison term by reinventing his autobiography and his ideology in the composition of *Mein Kampf*. A mix of contrived memoir and political *idées fixes* that was little read outside Nazi circles before 1930, the text is nevertheless an important guide to Hitler's racial beliefs and his political tactics. But political mobilization in Germany declined as the economy was salvaged and Germans made their peace with the status quo. A period of political and economic consolidation ensued, bringing slowly improving standards of living and consumption. For the scattered Nazis, power in Berlin was a receding horizon.

Weimar

As a traveller you might not choose to go from Munich to Berlin via Weimar; but for anyone who wants to understand the history of National Socialism in the 1920s, this notional itinerary has a compelling political logic. 'Weimar', as city and as metonym, allows us to project the currents of the 1920s onto a more intimate political scale.

The capital of the newly formed *Land* (state) of Thuringia, Weimar was the town that lent its name to the republican constitution, and then to the republic itself. It was here that the German national assembly retreated to draw up the constitution in February 1919, when revolutionary Berlin became too dangerous. Weimar was compact, bourgeois, and relatively calm (barracking a performance of Schiller's *Maria Stuart* was about the closest its citizens had come to revolution in November 1918); its famous National Theatre offered a convenient and secure location for the assembly's deliberations. The assembly eventually returned to the capital with its new constitution; but Weimar the city remained far more representative of Germany than Berlin ever was.

With 40,000 inhabitants, Weimar was larger than the communities in which most Germans lived in 1925, yet still small enough to typify these provincial small-town milieux. The local identities and sense of belonging they fostered remained hugely important, even as they coexisted with other markers of one's place in the world—religion, generation, gender, social status. The German language offers a richly layered term, *Heimat*—'homeland', the place and feeling of 'being at home'—to connote this sense of belonging to a familiar locality and an inherited social order. It conveys what might be called a 'socio-spatial' identity, a deeply imprinted mental map: as a Thuringian or a Bavarian, as a Nuremberger or Lübecker. It was through these smaller experiential units of identity and community, with their old geographical footprints and sentimental appeal, that most Germans understood their membership of the nation and responded to the political voices that claimed to represent it.

Weimar had one crucial distinction in this dense universe of German provincial communities. It enjoyed a unique status in the national imagination as the home of Goethe and Schiller, the supreme symbols of German cultural eminence. This legacy made it, no less than Berlin, an epicentre of the republic's culture wars and a microcosm of the political antagonisms that shook Germany in the 1920s and 1930s. Republicans enthusiastically co-opted Goethe and Schiller as the Enlightenment patrons of their democratic project. It was symbolic of this new order that, in 1919, the left-liberal Thuringian government made Weimar the home of that epitome of cultural innovation, Walter Gropius's Bauhaus design school. But the political turmoil of 1923 saw an attempted communist rising in the industrial centres of neighbouring Saxony as well as in Thuringia, which was suppressed only by the intervention of the Reichswehr (national army). Thereafter, politics in the *Land* and the city took a sharp turn to the right.

From 1924, Thuringia was ruled by right-wing governments that rolled back the progressive policies of their predecessors. The right tapped into widespread anxiety that local community values and national cultural identity were under threat from democrats and modernizers as well as the left; they reclaimed the city's grand intellectual legacy as the essence of traditional Germandom. So Weimar became a magnet for bourgeois antisemites and *völkisch* nationalists, and the city's commemoration of the 175th anniversary of Goethe's birth in 1924 was hijacked for a tasteless demonstration of their offensive views.

Unsurprisingly, Thuringia was the first state to lift the prohibition on the NSDAP after 1923, and one of the few German states never to ban Hitler himself from public speaking. Hitler liked Weimar and visited it dozens of times, staying at his favourite Hotel Elephant in the old town centre. His first public speech outside Bavaria was delivered in Weimar, in March 1925. The NSDAP assembled there regularly; it was where the foundation of the Hitler Youth was announced; where Hermann Göring met his wife, where Joseph Goebbels had his first breathless encounters with Hitler: 'Who is this man?' Goebbels asked his diary in October 1925. 'Half plebeian, half god! Is he really Christ, or only John [the Baptist]?'

It was in Weimar, too, that the Nazis held their first party rally after the failed putsch. Some 8,000 supporters gathered there in July 1926; they included a pantheon of bigwigs who were to become leading figures in the Nazi regime, among them Goebbels,

Hess, Himmler, Alfred Rosenberg, Wilhelm Frick, and Julius Streicher. For the first time, Hitler's recently established bodyguard, the SS, was on parade. The *Blutfahne*, the swastika flag stained and sacralized by the blood of the fourteen fallen 'heroes' killed in the attempted putsch of November 1923, made its first creepy appearance in Nazi ritual as SA men swore their oath of loyalty to Hitler. Bellicose speeches symbolically reclaimed the National Theatre from the republic; Jews and leftists were insulted and assaulted on the streets. The political repertoire of National Socialism was taking shape.

Weimar was, finally and sensationally, where the Nazis exercised ministerial power for the first time. Following dramatic gains in the Thuringian state elections at the end of 1929, the Nazis joined a coalition government in January 1930. At Hitler's insistence, his old ally Frick was given two key ministries, the interior and education, giving him control of the police and cultural policy. Frick made insolent use of the new cabinet's emergency powers. He effectively handed over the police force to Thuringia's thuggish Gauleiter (regional leader), Fritz Sauckel; he purged people and books from education and the arts; he bulldozed the appointment of an unqualified racist to a university chair in social anthropology. It would be hard to imagine a closer partnership between cultural and political belligerence—or a more precise foretaste of things to come. And so we return to our starting point. As Hitler had already come to realize, the political road to Berlin *did* run via 'Weimar': for it was only by means of the electoral law of the Weimar constitution, by winning votes, that the Nazis would be able to take power in Germany.

Hitler had learned this lesson in prison. As he told one of his visitors in 1924: 'Instead of working to achieve power by an armed coup, we shall have to hold our noses and enter the Reichstag... If out-voting them takes longer than out-shooting them, at least the results will be guaranteed by their own Constitution.' So the

Weimar constitution—that despised certificate of 'Jewish' democracy—had its uses after all. Its very legitimacy could become the ticket to a Nazi dictatorship in Berlin.

Berlin

Berlin, the capital of both Germany and the state of Prussia, was the antithesis of Weimar. Its four million inhabitants dwarfed Germany's other large cities, populating a metropolis that encapsulated everything the Nazis abominated. Like Prussia, it was ruled by a competent and effective democratic coalition, but to the Nazis, it was not just the corrupted capital of the detested republic but a stronghold of Bolshevism. To them it was an anomic, sexually deviant, Jewish megacity: an 'asphalt desert' that violated every fantasy of organic communitarianism and sentimental vision of *Heimat*. In Nazi eyes, Berlin's panoramic diversity and radical cultural creativity made it 'the melting pot of all evil...of prostitution, bars, sickness, movies, Marxism, Jews, strippers, Negro dances, and all the disgusting offspring of so-called modern art', as the Nazi *Völkischer Beobachter* newspaper put it in 1929. But it was also the city on which the party had to train its sights in the quest for power.

Consolidation

With some difficulty, Hitler recovered leadership of the scattered and demoralized Nazi Party in the mid-1920s and worked to rebuild it. Like most fringe political parties, the NSDAP was prone to splits and secessions, but Hitler managed to beat off successive challenges and to assert the primacy of his absolute leadership over programme and principles. The party rebuilt itself for political mobilization rather than insurrection. The SA was demoted from an armed militia to a rowdy political support troop, and Hitler gathered round him a cadre of comrades whose loyalty matched his trust, including most of the party's Gauleiters. The essential trappings of the Führer cult were adopted: the adulatory language, the 'Heil Hitler!' greeting and salute, the presumptuous identification of Hitler with Germany's coming redemption.

In the mid-1920s, the yield of this new strategy was sparse if measured by Hitler's new standard of electoral success. With economic stabilization and a retreat from confrontational politics on the far right and left, the republic was consolidated and was able to blunt revolutionary impulses with major legislative programmes in social policy and industrial relations. The NSDAP was marginal and seemed a spent political force. It averaged less than 4 per cent of the total vote in local and state elections between December 1924 and 1928, and even less in the Reichstag elections of 1928, when, despite an energetic campaign, Nazi representation fell to just twelve seats out of 491. But in the shadow of this electoral feebleness, the Nazi Party was on the path to less spectacular but significant achievements. Membership grew from 35,000 in 1926 to 129,000 in 1930, bringing a welcome influx of funds and a concomitant growth in the network of local party branches: in Bavaria alone, from 139 in 1925 to 776 in 1930. Overseeing this grassroots expansion was the party's newly bureaucratized Munich HQ, backed by a growing corps of trained speakers and functionaries (Figure 2). Hitler's identification with the party was becoming seared into its public image, and National Socialists nursed their dreams of future greatness. 'German politics is increasingly taking note of us', Goebbels claimed in July 1926, not long after his appointment as Gauleiter in Berlin. 'Pitying smiles are turning to mockery, mockery to slander, slander to terror...Today we are beginning to be feared again.'

Opportunity

These were the foundations on which the party was able to build its nationwide support after 1929, when first the economic and then the political stability of the republic tipped into crisis. Goebbels's boast was premature, but local and regional elections in 1929 did yield evidence—as we have seen in Thuringia—that

2. The membership record room of the Brown House, the prestigious NSDAP headquarters opened in a fashionable district of Munich in 1931. Its office space enabled the party to keep abreast of its rapid growth and increasingly elaborate organizational structure.

the NSDAP was beginning to make serious advances. As the economic depression bit deeper, industrial production in 1932 sank to little more than half what it had been before 1929; agriculture was in crisis, the banking system was wavering, public finances were in tatters, and registered unemployment rose to six million, with young people especially hard hit. Behind the bare figures lay a welfare system in free fall, families with no one in work, undernourished children, pensioners begging in the streets, unemployed workers tramping the roads.

The economic crisis deepened into a systemic political crisis as the national and *Länder* governments attempted, with narrowing party support and decreasing public confidence, to cope with the Depression and its shattering but unevenly distributed social and political impacts. Employers resisted pressure to fund the collapsing unemployment insurance system, and looked for political defenders against militant workers and the parties of the left. Successive national cabinets, unable to command majorities in an increasingly divided and paralysed Reichstag, resorted to rule by presidential decree. The mayors of big cities like Leipzig or Dortmund used the fiscal crisis to grab executive power and marginalize their elected councils. At every level, the ebbing of confidence in democratic government was palpable.

Another reason for the atrophy of democratic government was that the Nazi Party suddenly and unexpectedly wrestled its way into the centre of German politics, where it adopted a stance of aggressive obstructionism. In the national elections called in September 1930 by chancellor Heinrich Brüning, in the misguided calculation that he could decimate the SPD and secure Reichstag support for his government, the Nazi Party won a stunning 107 seats with nearly six and a half million votes. Thuringia was not the only state where the NSDAP made inroads into regional and local government, giving them additional vantage points from which to disrupt democratic proceedings and spread their message. Meanwhile the party's expansion continued: its membership reached almost a million in 1932, and its 12,000 local branches gave the Nazis a national network unrivalled by any other party on the right.

The electoral and organizational growth of the Nazi movement parallels the statistics of Germany's economic collapse so neatly that it is tempting to say that the Depression delivered Germany to the Nazis. This is not wrong, but on its own it ducks the hard questions. Why was NSDAP the beneficiary of the crisis? Who supported the Nazis after 1929, and why? Contemporaries and historians alike found it difficult to answer these questions, because, although analysis of membership and electoral records can help identify the social profile and scale of support, the crucial question of motivation remains harder to pin down. In fact, dismayed contemporaries found it difficult to believe that this movement could capture the support of so many Germans—with its crude ideology and systematically mendacious propaganda, its demands for national discipline and unity that were belied by its own public rowdiness and history of internal splits, its strutting leader who appeared ludicrous to many. They insisted that the Nazi Party was at its core inauthentic, that it did not really represent the interests of ordinary Germans as it claimed. Either its leaders were cynically bent on power for themselves or else their party was the creature of powerful elites who were secretly financing it for their own purposes—principally, as a weapon to keep the left at bay. These claims carry weight, but historians have dismantled the image of deluded or supine masses that they also implied, and have proposed explanations of the movement's appeal to its members and voters which may seem more mundane but are also more attentive to the historical evidence.

One answer to the first question has been suggested already. In the mid-1920s, the Nazi Party had prepared itself to launch an unprecedented political offensive when the opportunity arose. Once the Depression hit, the party machine was able to rapidly exploit the new situation. The Nazis' initial efforts to entice blue-collar workers away from the left had been less successful than they had anticipated, but the party now found itself gaining unexpected support in rebellious rural communities and small towns hit by Brüning's deeply resented poll tax (the *Bürgersteuer*). Its leaders accordingly shifted their strategy to appeal to a more middle-class electorate who had no love for a republic that seemed to frustrate their ambitions and to offer no political protection for their interests: anxious farmers, craftsmen and shop-owners, university students facing unemployment, civil servants suffering salary cuts, status-conscious professionals, nervous pensioners, women bypassed by the promise of emancipation. Many of these voters had something to lose—status, prospects, savings—and fading confidence that the republic would protect them. Proportionally more of the Nazi Party's new support after 1929 came from these middle-class groups than from the working class, and more from Protestant than Catholic milieux; men outnumbered women; young men under 30 were especially drawn to an inspiring national cause, making up half the membership before 1933. Although there was a high turnover in membership, the alternative of supporting the hapless middle-class political parties was increasingly unattractive. The Nazis harvested voters' insecurity and cultural unease, as well as their hopes that an outsider party with a galvanizing political presence could deliver something genuinely new to Germany.

By contrast with the Nazis' own appearance of energetic mobilization, the muddier profiles and weaker organizational bases of competing parties looked increasingly unimpressive. In the last month of the 1930 Reichstag election campaign, the NSDAP mounted an unparalleled offensive of 34,000 meetings across Germany, while Hitler's speeches attracted huge audiences—16,000 in Berlin, perhaps twice that in Breslau. Even these figures were dwarfed in the feverish campaigns of 1932, when national, state, and presidential elections followed quickly on one another, and the country seemed to be saturated in Nazi propaganda.

The contents of this propaganda barrage were short on specific policies, but long on relentless exposures of the mounting economic devastation, on brazen exploitation of popular anxieties, and exaggerated attacks on the corruption and incompetence of what the Nazis now called 'the Weimar system'. Nazi speakers insisted that the sources of national recovery lay in familiar and shared values of ethnic community and national unity, of collective endeavour and the ordered family—but that this needed new energy and leadership. For the first time, imagery of Hitler's private life as a man of modest and orderly domestic habits was invoked to bolster his public standing. This simultaneously reassuring and inspiring message exercised considerable electoral appeal. Its promise could be contrasted with the left's confrontational language of class, and with the scourge of social and political fragmentation that had allegedly rendered Germany a prey to its enemies within and without.

The promise to save Germany from class war was a winning tactic in the Nazis' appeal to middle-class and rural voters, condensing social democracy and communism into a single 'Marxist' spectre. Hitler now played down antisemitism in his public speeches, even if other party mouthpieces—Goebbels's newspaper *Der Angriff,* Streicher's virulent *Der Stürmer*—persisted in the racist language that remained core to the party's internal identity. The messages purveyed by its speakers were in fact not so different from those of other right-wing parties, but the Nazis insisted that they were not just another political party, but a dynamic and dedicated movement (*Bewegung*), commanded not by a dusty politician but by a resolute and inspirational leader who was also a man of the people. In the 1932 presidential elections, this promise of salvationist leadership was still successfully claimed by the existing president, the war hero Hindenburg, who beat Hitler soundly in the final round. But in the parliamentary elections three months later, when Brüning's patrician successor Franz von Papen took his own gamble with the polls, the Nazis were astonishingly successful. With over 37 per cent of the vote, they took 230 seats and became by far the largest party in the deeply divided Reichstag, where active support for the republic was collapsing.

The Nazis capitalized on a widespread loss of confidence in the political system, a sense that republican pluralism had failed. Their propaganda vilified and derided all of the republic's political parties, whose sheer number—a baroque total of sixty-two contested the July 1932 Reichstag elections—was a persuasive weapon in the Nazis' unremitting mockery of democracy. Whereas each of these other parties allegedly appealed to one class or sectional interest alone, Nazi propaganda enumerated what the party offered to every social group in turn, while also insisting that only the NSDAP represented and united all of them, irrespective of status, occupation, or religion. With the first breakthroughs to the Catholic and women's vote and growing working-class support, the Nazi Party could project itself as something hitherto unseen in the republic's class-driven politics: a movement of

all Germans, irrespective of class or *Stand*—ostensibly the
Volksgemeinschaft of the future in embryonic form.

The NSDAP also trumpeted itself as the only major party that
had never held national office, never been in coalition with the
'November criminals', never implicated itself in the Weimar
'system'. Despite the fact that by mid-1932 the party had in fact
joined governing coalitions in four *Länder*, while its deputies
were doing their best to wreck orderly proceedings in the
Reichstag, its spokesmen proclaimed that the Nazis bore no
responsibility for the crisis. They alone had the clean hands, the
backing, and the willpower to purge Germany of all its ills,
starting with democracy itself.

Velocity and urgency were integral to the Nazi Party's self-image:
'Tempo! Tempo! that was the motto for our work', wrote Goebbels
in the heat of the 1932 campaigns. Yet its capacity to mobilize its
supporters risks projecting a misleading image of unstoppability,
and does not explain its final climb to power. For, even though
national voting rates reached well over 80 per cent in 1932,
political power in Germany did not reside exclusively in the ballot
box. This never delivered the NSDAP an overall majority, and
between the July and November 1932 Reichstag elections the party
even lost two million votes, undermining its image of inexorable
advance. But because elections did not produce working majorities
in the Reichstag, the shape and fate of Germany's government
were increasingly determined by elite machination rather than
democratic process.

Endgame

As the political system buckled, access to power was traded within
the political establishment and the industrial and agrarian elites,
along circuits veiled from public scrutiny but centred on the
offices of the octogenarian president Hindenburg and the last two
chancellors before Hitler—the Catholic grandee Papen and his

successor, the military grey eminence Kurt von Schleicher. The democratic republic itself was under threat as right-wing politicians plotted constitutional revisions that were intended to replace it with an explicitly authoritarian system of presidential rule capable of crushing the left. Papen's dismissal of Prussia's left-liberal government on a flimsy constitutional pretext in July 1932, and its replacement by executive rule, were shocking omens of this.

The NSDAP was implicated on both sides of this paradoxical coexistence of mass mobilization below and constitutional attenuation above, along with a crucial third element: the threat of a violent seizure of power. The politics of violence had never disappeared from the Nazi movement, but only shifted from insurrection to murderous attacks on the Nazis' communist and social democrat enemies. SA detachments engaged in demonstrations of political intimidation that regularly tipped over into street battles with the left's paramilitaries; in the early 1930s, hundreds were killed and thousands injured on both sides. SA men were young and aggressive. They epitomized physically the party's hyper-masculinist mythology of youth, will, struggle, and martyrdom, and they spearheaded its growing reputation as the only force capable of resisting Bolshevism in Germany. Spurred on by its leadership, the SA also represented the NSDAP's own 'left'. Its rank and file, many of them unemployed, took seriously the radical promises implied by the words 'socialist' and 'workers' in their party's name; they were increasingly impatient for the revolutionary overthrow of capitalism as well as the republic, and for their share in the spoils.

With power apparently within the Nazi Party's grasp by mid-1932, Hitler was forced into a balancing act between the competing demands of mobilizing the party faithful, holding together a multifarious and undependable electorate, negotiating with Germany's political and economic elites, and facing down increasingly mutinous unrest in the 300,000-strong SA. Hitler's skill in juggling these pressures was inflated in later mythology, but among his key weapons was the veiled threat that he could not control his restless revolutionary ranks if the Nazis were not allowed into power on his terms. Another was the persuasive claim that his party represented the nation as no other could, certainly not Papen's patrician 'cabinet of the barons'.

After the Nazi Party suffered a significant loss of votes in the November 1932 national elections, Papen's successor Schleicher tried unsuccessfully to lure a segment of its membership away from Hitler. But when, two months later, the NSDAP recovered its electoral momentum in the small state of Lippe-Detmold, the beleaguered elites knew that they needed the party's mass strength in order to legitimate their own coup against the republic and the left. Reluctant though they were to give Hitler the chancellorship as the price of his cooperation, they worried that time was not on their side. The political value of the Nazis would shrink if their mass support were to waver again and the democratic defenders of the republic recover their confidence.

In January 1933, the political situation in Berlin resembled an upside-down replay of November 1923 in Munich: Germany's political establishment plotting to exploit the Nazis as a tool for their coup against the republic, the fired-up Nazi rank and file straining for the putsch that would deliver Germany into its own hands, Hitler anticipating his summons to high office. Germany's political elites were confident that, in Papen's cynical words, they were about to 'hire Hitler' as a political strongman for their own destructive purposes. After knife-edge negotiations with Papen, the DNVP, and Hindenburg, Hitler achieved his goal of the chancellorship, though at a price. He was forced to accept a cabinet dominated by powerful conservative nationalists, including Papen, the DNVP leader Alfred Hugenberg, and Stahlhelm leader Franz Seldte. On 30 January 1933, Hindenburg swore Hitler in as chancellor of the Weimar Republic. Just two other leading Nazis—Frick and Göring—joined the cabinet of the new National

Government, with Göring also taking over the Prussian interior ministry—including, crucially, its police force. That was all; but it was to be enough.

That same day, a Hamburg schoolteacher, Luise Solmitz, recorded the appeal of the new ministerial line-up to middle-class Nazi sympathizers like herself: 'What a cabinet!!' she wrote in her diary. 'Hitler, Hugenberg, Seldte, Papen!!! On each hangs a large part of my hopes for Germany…It is so unbelievably wonderful that I must write it down quickly before the first discordant note comes.' A day later, we already can catch that note in Goebbels's diary: 'The first stage! The struggle continues! Hugenberg…Papen vice-chancellor. Seldte labour minister. These are flaws. Must be rubbed out.'

Most Germans would have had little reason to believe that this new coalition would prove any more durable than its immediate predecessors; few could have predicted that, within months, Goebbels's hopes would have been fulfilled, and Solmitz's optimism shattered.

Chapter 4
Power

The Nazi leadership was ill-prepared for the exercise of state power. The pre-1933 party had been dedicated primarily to gaining power through mass mobilization and the disruption of democratic government. Its leaders were held together by personal loyalty to their Führer, and their political beliefs coexisted loosely rather than sharing ideological coherence. These qualities served their purpose during the Nazi Party's race for power, but they were unpropitious for mastering the tasks of government. The style of rule that developed after 1933 was less a monolithic totalitarianism than a hybrid dictatorship mingling three sources of power: the inherited state system; the extra-legal terror of the police and SS; and the personal status of the Führer. The regime was parasitic on existing governmental institutions, notably the bureaucracies on whose expertise, despite Nazi odium, the formal conduct of state business relied. With control over the police—the all-important source of power in a dictatorship—Himmler was able to extract it as well as the SS from the state and its laws, and to conduct his terror regime in a realm of unregulated prerogative power. Finally, the person of the Führer supposedly incarnated the unity of the *Volk* and dominated the regime as the supreme and uncontested source of all authority.

Taking power, 1933–1934

If totalitarian power eluded the Nazi regime, dictatorship did not. One of the chief buttresses for its construction was the fact that so much of the spadework had already been accomplished by its predecessors—as if the chickens had prepared their coop for the arrival of the fox. Hitler was invited into the new National Government on the rubble of a republic whose constitutional foundations and political culture had already been deeply undermined as power was deliberately tugged into the executive after 1930. Hitler's elite collaborators had scripted him to solve their crisis of control by lending leadership and a popular mandate to an authoritarian government, but otherwise trusting that he could be kept on the political sidelines. Hitler fulfilled the first part of the bargain in the spring of 1933 with the Nazis' crushing assault on the KPD and SPD (still hamstrung by mutual hostility) and on the trade unions; its speed and violence left their members in shocked disarray. But although Hitler's backers held stronger cards, they were also unable to grasp that, with their own connivance, the rules of the political game were being transformed. After the first tactical compromises, there would be no leadership role for them in the new Nazi universe. On the contrary, Hitler was able to advance his own ambitions behind the reassuring cover provided by his political and military collaborators, from president Hindenburg down.

In this damaged and dishonest political environment, the Nazi capture of political power in 1933–4—the process by which Hitler's leadership of a coalition government was transformed into the Nazi regime—was neither coup nor revolution, but nor was it a legitimate succession. In the history books, it has become known as the *Machtergreifung*, 'seizure of power'; but at the time Nazis and nationalists alike described it as an orderly 'takeover of power' (*Machtübernahme*) or a unifying 'national rising' (*nationale Erhebung*). Yet all these terms indicate that something more fundamental than a change of government was set in motion in January 1933. Behind the façade of legitimacy, the structures of representative democracy, political pluralism, and civil liberties were to be quickly dismantled. The Nazi leadership was about to transform power into tyranny.

Some combination of an attempted electoral mandate, powers to suppress political disorder, and the grant of extra-parliamentary authority had become the norm for each new government since 1930, but this time with a crucial difference. Unlike his predecessors, Hitler was accorded unfettered rights of executive government, shorn of any presidential or Reichstag oversight, as well as access to sweeping police powers of 'protective custody' (*Schutzhaft*) without trial or appeal. In the run-up to new national elections—and in an uncanny physical anticipation of the Nazis' own political intentions—the Reichstag was destroyed by arson on 27 February in circumstances that remain murky today. A hastily drafted but far-reaching emergency decree, known in abbreviation as the 'Reichstag Fire Decree', immediately suspended all constitutional civil rights and handed over powers of summary arrest to the police. It also empowered the Reich government to take over—to usurp—the government of any *Land* failing to protect 'public safety and order'.

Despite the emerging conditions of repression and terror licensed by this decree, the Nazi–nationalist coalition won only a bare majority in the 5 March elections, while the combined vote for the SPD and KPD was an impressive 22 million (Figure 3). Procedural sleight of hand was therefore required to achieve the two-thirds Reichstag majority required by the constitution for a crucial emergency law known as an Enabling Act (*Ermächtigungsgesetz*). This superficially legitimate act gave the chancellor and his cabinet summary power to enact laws and amend the constitution. With the communists in custody, in hiding, or already in exile, the Catholic Centre Party bribed with promises of respect for Christian values and the Catholic church, and the liberal

In grösster Not
Adolf Hitler zum
wählt auch

wählte Hindenburg
Reichskanzler,
Jhr Liste 1.

3. Chancellor Hitler channels the beneficent aura of President Hindenburg in a poster for the 5 March 1933 Reichstag elections. 'In time of greatest need, Hindenburg chose Adolf Hitler as chancellor; now you too choose List 1 [NSDAP].'

parties reduced to a handful of shell-shocked representatives, the only votes against it on 23 March were cast by the ninety-four SPD deputies. As Goebbels exulted in his diary the following day, 'Now we are masters of Germany under the constitution as well.' Thus was Hitler's cynical promise of 1924 vindicated.

Yet who precisely constituted Goebbels's 'we' was problematic. Hitler's chancellorship on its own could not guarantee immediate Nazi power over Germany's elaborate constitutional system, its political, economic, and military institutions, elite networks, and bureaucratic hierarchies, let alone its dense and intricate civil society. To achieve 'mastery' required an initial balancing act between political caution and assertive momentum: between tactical compromises with political, military, and economic elites, and a more brutal monopolization—*Gleichschaltung*, or 'coordination'—of the public sphere. Freedom from this constraint was attained only through a series of tense showdowns between 1934 and 1938 that enabled Hitler to survive incipient moves against him and to drive major establishment figures out of government. At the same time, old tensions within the Nazi movement were exposed and new fault-lines opened up: fractured relationships between central authority and local ambition, between organs of the party and the state, and between freelance violence and state-sponsored terror.

The SA 'putsch', 1934

The activities and fate of the SA in 1933/4 offer an instructive microcosm of these dynamics. Stormtroopers took a prominent and rowdy role in enforcing the nationwide boycott of Jewish-owned businesses on 1 April 1933—the first national action organized by Goebbels in his newly created role as minister for public enlightenment and propaganda. More important, the SA's dedication to violence and thirst for revenge against their political adversaries radicalized the state-sanctioned campaign of police terror that bludgeoned the organized left into submission in the spring and summer of 1933 and sent many into exile. In Prussia, with Göring in command of the police, SA men were sworn in en masse as police auxiliaries. Throughout Germany, tens of thousands of communists and social democrats were seized, beaten up, taken into 'protective custody', and thrown into prison or improvised concentration camps: the first of these was set up on 3 March in Nohra, near Weimar, by SA, Stahlhelm, and SS squads. In hundreds of such sites across Germany, largely inaccessible to the rule of law, male detainees were subjected to appalling violence and cruelty, and at least a hundred murdered; anyone who was also Jewish drew particular abuse; women detainees were not immune from mistreatment. Although most were released after a few terrifying weeks or months, the cumulative total had reached at least 100,000 by the end of 1933, effectively decapitating opposition from the left. There was little public disquiet at the repression of these 'Marxist' enemies and little secrecy about the existence of the camps, which were successfully publicized as sites of harsh but well-deserved corrective discipline for communist traitors.

The SA's contribution to the organized terror was crucial, but it was also symptomatic of the freelance localism of the Nazi takeover, which threatened to fragment into hundreds of disorderly seizures of power in towns and cities across the land. Hitler was concerned that ongoing lawlessness, even if mainly targeted against unpopular communists and Jews, would jeopardize the fragile balance of his cabinet, endanger economic recovery, and repel the ranks of his conservative-nationalist supporters. Worse, the SA rank and file, incited by their ambitious leader Ernst Röhm, believed that they were acting as the armed vanguard of a promised political and economic 'second revolution', an aspiration echoed among the millions of unemployed. By mid-1934, conservative leaders, notably vice-chancellor Papen, were openly expressing alarm at the lawless elements of Nazi rule, and public resentment of SA impunity was mounting. With the general staff branding the

4.5 million-strong troop an intolerable threat to the Reichswehr's monopoly, the Nazi–nationalist coalition was vulnerable.

Starting on the night of 30 June 1934, Hitler took action to resolve this growing crisis with an astonishingly brazen gamble that came to be known as the 'Night of the Long Knives'. Röhm and prominent SA leaders were shot by SS squads backed by Reichswehr units; a number of inconvenient opposition figures were also murdered or arrested. This gangster-like liquidation of over a hundred men and several women was retrospectively legalized; it was successfully represented by Hitler in public as a bold act of 'self-defence' against corruption and high treason, which had prevented a greater bloodbath (it helped that Röhm's homosexuality could also be used to smear his name). Public anger with the SA was alleviated; relations with the military were stabilized, and conservatives and business interests were reassured, if equivocally. Hitler's authority was sealed. The decapitated SA lost its leadership role, although it remained a school of German masculinity. But with this, Himmler's SS was launched into an impregnable position.

Like the repression of the left, the 'Night of the Long Knives' affirmed that extrajudicial violence was integral to the exercise of Nazi power, yet also not unwelcome to much of the nation; the critical question was who wielded it, and against whom. It also displayed Hitler's ability to breach every convention of political conduct and get away with it. But a functional state and economy, the prerequisite for his overriding agenda of rearmament and war, could not rest on terror alone. It needed not only popular legitimacy, but a degree of structural stability: something the 'Third Reich' struggled to sustain.

The Nazi state

The Nazi state has been described as a permanent state of emergency. The Weimar constitution was never repealed, and the new state emerged piecemeal from the exceptional powers handed over in February and March 1933. Its domination was increasingly exerted through prerogative authority that sidestepped legal norms and procedures and shattered the rule of law. The Nazis, steeped in the myth of their movement's capacity to master world-historical tasks by audacious leadership and will alone, were contemptuous of the legal niceties and cautious procedures of the state, its laws, and its officials, which they saw primarily as obstacles to be swept aside. 'These people really have no idea what a state is', wrote the conservative diplomat Ulrich von Hassell in 1939. Against a powerful tradition in German political thought, Nazi ideology held that it was not the state but the nation, the *Volk*, that was the rationale and purpose of all political endeavour.

The procedures of the state could nevertheless be used to remake it. A torrent of enactments siphoned political authority upwards and inwards, erecting the semblance of a newly centralized, unified German state while also distributing power to new authorities outside it. Democratic self-government was eradicated at every level. The hapless political parties were soon banned or dissolved themselves, leaving the NSDAP the sole legal party by July 1933. The Reichstag was reduced to a ceremonial nonentity, with some of its authority vacuumed into a new law on plebiscites. Wags called it the highest-paid men's choir in Germany, because its all-male membership met once a year to sing the national anthem and then went home. Simultaneously, the civil service and judiciary were purged of political dissenters and Jews; as bureaucratic impartiality and judicial independence were eviscerated, officials clutched at fig-leaf rationales to hide their naked complicity with the regime.

By 1935, a programme of structural reforms piloted by Frick's interior ministry relieved the *Länder* of their constitutions and sovereignty and reduced them to subordinate administrations overseen by Nazi Gauleiters in a new role as 'Reichsstatthalter' (state commissioners). The police system was on its way to becoming an independent and politicized terror apparatus under the command of the SS leader, Himmler, and new special courts (Sondergerichte) were established for the trial of political offences and treason. Yet, in the midst of these profound transformations of state power and assaults on the rule of law, a familiar dimension of formal regulations and everyday procedures, of apparent rule *by* law persisted. This side of the 'dual state', perceptively analysed at the time by Ernst Fraenkel, persuaded numerous public officials and ordinary Germans that the powers claimed by the new regime were, despite everything, legitimate.

These changes aimed at comprehensive political concentration and administrative consolidation, but although one-party rule did away with the alleged defects of republican pluralism, it imposed new strains on the functional capacity of the state. Now elevated onto the stage of government, rivalrous party chiefs asserted their right to interfere directly in official decisions and bureaucratic processes, and exploited their status as Nazi 'old fighters' (*alte Kämpfer*) to get preferential access to Hitler. Their ambitions were met by Hitler's preference for establishing ever more special agencies and commissions, especially for tasks of economic mobilization; these bypassed existing authorities and hierarchies and were headed by comrades answerable to him alone. Insiders deplored these innovations as a profound threat to the coherence and efficiency of bureaucratic government and economic planning (one senior civil servant described the result as 'organized chaos'). At the same time, the young careerists who staffed the new agencies kept the system going by devising innovative techniques of management that worked round, rather than through, the clogged bureaucratic channels of the state.

These developments are not mere footnotes to the history of Nazi dictatorship, but help to answer one of the questions that has perplexed contemporaries and historians: how a modern, professionally governed state like Germany became entangled in the Nazis' utopian and ultimately apocalyptic projects of imperialism and genocide. The most influential answers have highlighted the regime's combination of self-sustaining and self-destructive tendencies: the inordinate ambitions of totalitarian domination; Hitler's charismatic status and phantasmic ideology; the abrasive coexistence of a normative bureaucratic state with a realm of unregulated prerogative power; the reckless and corrupting radicalization as rivals outbid each other in the race for favour and power. Whatever their different emphases, all interpretations have to focus on the primary relationship between ideology and structure: between Hitler the Führer and the regime he dominated.

The Führer state

A month after the SA coup, on 1 August 1934, Hindenburg made his final contribution to the Nazi regime by dying. As he faded, the presidency was summarily abolished and its powers, including the supreme command of the armed forces, were transferred into Hitler's new office of 'Führer and Reich Chancellor'. Hitler's new status was approved in a plebiscite on 19 August, and if it was not quite as unanimous as the Nazi leadership had expected, the result confirmed Hitler's unconditional personal power. Just as he had come to personify the party's salvationist mission in its time of struggle, so Hitler was now said to embody the authentic unity and destiny of the *Volk*. This almost metaphysical proposition bypassed the intermediate institutions of party and state, and endowed Hitler with an aura detached from the rest of the Nazi regime. 'In the Führer the existential laws of the *Volk* manifest themselves', wrote one expert in constitutional law, while Gauleiter Hans Schemm proclaimed that 'Hitler speaks as the personification of the German people...Hitler and Germany...represent a single unity'. These extravagant attempts to capture Hitler's political status were echoed in the ludicrous adulation from his entourage and in the trust lodged in him by ordinary Germans. At the same time, Hitler was aware of the real strains on this idealized relationship with the German *Volk*, and he was never more popular than when he was able to snatch stunning foreign policy successes from the brink of war.

The imagery of Hitler's absolute personal authority had to be carefully manipulated—this was Goebbels's job—to ensure that only Hitler was credited with the regime's successes, and only others held responsible for its failures. The question of whom to blame for failure in a dictatorship is always tricky. Crucial for the Nazi regime was to point the finger at alleged external and internal enemies, a label unrelentingly inflicted on 'international Jewry' and Bolshevism. But the 'Führer myth', staged publicly in the great party rallies and ceremonial broadcast speeches that bound Führer and followers in an embrace of mutual recognition, also came into play. It projected the Führer as the incarnation of the popular needs and fantasies vested in him, elevating the figure above his regime and protecting him from the defects and failures of its lesser representatives. This was the essence of the charismatic power relationship described in Chapter 1.

Hitler's status was not merely a personality cult, but was also anchored in the anti-egalitarian and anti-democratic political concepts of the 'personality principle' and 'leadership principle' that he had first elaborated in *Mein Kampf*. The exceptional self-activating personality who won recognition as leader by his own genius was ostensibly the antithesis of the parliamentary politician hobbled by his homogenized electoral majority. The 'leadership principle' was its counterpart, stipulating that authority ran from the top down and responsibility from the bottom up. These precepts hardly amounted to a theory of politics, but they saturated the political vocabulary and the hierarchical structure of party and government after 1933.

Hitler's absolute authority after 1933 was not only exerted through his direct power of command (or refusal). Equally important was that his subordinates sought his personal mandate to legitimate their own decisions, as well as to boost their standing among competitors for power. Whether or not Hitler choreographed a deliberately competitive instability to enhance his own dominion—a matter on which historians disagree—this dynamic radically dislocated the conduct of government after 1933. Access to Hitler—literally, gaining entry to his presence—became decisive. This was easier for Hitler's most trusted party comrades, who could meet him face-to-face in his conversational evenings or at Nazi Party events. The work of ministers and civil servants, by contrast, was impeded by Hitler's repudiation of established bureaucratic procedure and collective decision-making (cabinet meetings withered and finally vanished in 1938), and his reliance on his own instincts. 'I know if one of my decisions or actions is right', he explained to Hess. 'At that moment I can't yet say why, but I feel that it is right and developments will prove its rightness.'

The most consequential effect of the combination of Hitler's supreme responsibility with his cavalier approach to decision-making was that it fostered what might be called a politics of anticipatory fulfilment or political pre-emption. Hitler indulged his providential visions in rhetorical gestures and digressions, rather than in orderly instructions; he was also prone to irresolution, to 'choosing not to choose' until his 'instinct' took over. Subordinates filled the gaps between the broad ideological frameworks he laid down and the political conclusions that could be drawn from them, thereby propelling policy forward with an almost self-acting momentum. With their bureaucracies, they 'work[ed] towards the Führer', as one Nazi official put it in 1934, in a phrase that has come to encapsulate the regime's cumulative drive. We will encounter this dynamic at its most devastating in the crystallization of anti-Jewish policy during the war.

The SS and police state

Brute force saturated and sustained the Nazi political system. Neither Hitler's dictatorship nor his most radical policies would have been possible without one of the most fateful shifts in the distribution of power after 1933. This was the takeover of the German police and security forces by Heinrich Himmler and their alignment with the SS, through which the SS was transformed into the most powerful and dreaded organization in the 'Third Reich'. This transformation represented virtually a second, creeping seizure of power. It foreshadowed a comprehensive system of terror that would not only anticipate and neutralize alleged threats to the body politic, but also justify the powerful security apparatus this demanded.

The SS *was* the Nazi terror state, in that it was the supreme institutional embodiment of prerogative power and the rule of exception imposed by force. It achieved a position outside legal control and ethical norms, and operated across the political spectrum from the policing of everyday life to top-secret projects of mass murder. With Hitler's endorsement, Himmler inserted the SS as a para-state agency into those fields of policy and action that they deemed beyond the capacity of even the Nazified German state. Its role in the massacre of SA leaders in July 1934 was an early example that was crucial to cementing the power of the SS; but it was soon to be massively exceeded by the SS's leading role in racial war and genocide.

When Himmler had taken command in 1929, the SS was a tiny subsidiary of the SA tasked with guarding Hitler. Inspired by murky visions of a future Teutonic-Nordic warrior community, Himmler expanded the SS and recast it as a racial and ideological elite, a quasi-religious order bound in personal fealty to himself and Hitler, and dedicated to values of loyalty and—Himmler's repeated watchword—'decency'. His own unimpressive persona, his insecurity and bizarre beliefs were compensated for by an obsessive attention to bureaucratic detail that gave him the edge over less meticulous rivals. His indispensable right-hand man from 1931 was the coldly ambitious Reinhard Heydrich, who took charge of what became the SS surveillance and security arm, the

SD (Sicherheitsdienst). These elements—a cultish elitism, fetishistic loyalty, and bureaucratic management—were early indications of how SS power would develop.

When Hitler named Himmler 'Reichsführer SS und Chef der Deutschen Polizei' in June 1936, the appointment crowned his gradual takeover of the police in every German state since 1933. Under Heydrich, the SD became the leading edge of Himmler's vision of a single national security system, merged with the SS, freed from state control, and operating outside normal legal constraints. Himmler increasingly saw this as a crusade against 'organized subhumanity', a phobic offensive against those identified as subversive, deviant, and alien. A major step was taken with the establishment in September 1939 of the Reich Security Main Office (Reichssicherheitshauptamt), henceforth the amalgamated agency of SS terror in Germany and occupied Europe.

The RSHA included the Gestapo (secret state police), the principal instrument for the repressive policing of dissent, subversion, racial offences, and social nonconformity. Antecedents of the Gestapo had led the round-up of the regime's political opponents in 1933, and it was largely successful in suppressing organized resistance thereafter. The Gestapo's relatively small and dispersed workforce (a total of some 7,000 in 1937) meant that its work depended on the local cooperation of Nazi Party authorities and a network of informants, as well as denunciations from the general public. It cultivated an image of all-seeing omnipotence that considerably exceeded the reality; but it also benefited from its fearsome and deserved reputation for extreme brutality, which extorted levels of compliance well beyond what it could directly impose.

The other instruments of repression, the concentration camps, were taken under SS control in 1934 (Map 1). Since most political detainees had been released by then, some government figures argued that the emergency was over, and that the beefed-up courts and prison system could henceforth cope with the

Map 1. Concentration camps in Germany before the war.

repression of political opponents (and until 1942/3, the regular
prisons held more inmates than the concentration camps). But
the camps and extrajudicial detention were integral to Himmler's
envisaged SS security system. In 1936, with Hitler's endorsement,
he began the construction of an expanded network for incarcerating
the population of 'organized subhumanity'. New camps were
modelled largely on the camp Himmler had established in March
1933 in Dachau, near Munich, with its brutally calibrated regime
of degradation, correctional work, and terror. Dachau was now

expanded, and further camps constructed at Sachsenhausen and, for women, Ravensbrück. With Gauleiter Sauckel's enthusiastic backing, another large camp for men was built near Weimar on the Ettersberg, a wooded hill once frequented by Goethe and since then a favourite excursion spot. Bowing to local objections, the camp was given another name, Buchenwald, that spared citizens' cultural sensibilities.

Opened in 1937, Buchenwald was soon integrated in the local economy; it was served by transport links and public utilities, and was generally accepted as necessary for the security of the *Volksgemeinschaft*. The camp held thousands of 'habitual' and 'hereditary' criminals, 'work-shy' and 'asocial' detainees, and Jewish 'offenders' rounded up in mass arrest sweeps in 1937 and 1938. It was also the temporary holding-pen for 10,000 of the Jewish men seized in the November 1938 pogrom (see Chapter 5), and it held its share of the other designated enemies of the Nazi state: political prisoners, Jehovah's Witnesses, and homosexuals. The SS ruled all their fiefs with cruelty, caprice, and corruption. They delegated much of the lower-level management of the camp to 'kapos', prisoner functionaries, an abusive system that added to prisoners' miseries, although it could be turned against itself. In Buchenwald, the 'politicals' managed to gain control by mid-1938 and established an effective underground resistance that protected communist inmates in particular.

The establishment of the new camps was accompanied by a more systematic exploitation of their economic potential than hitherto, supervised by Oswald Pohl, head of the SS's economic and construction offices. Himmler had cultivated relations with leading industrialists since 1936, with the aim of extending SS influence and raising funds for SS expansion. The SS's own economic activities took off from 1938, when Himmler seized the chance to enhance its power with a major new initiative: the use of inmate labour to supply construction materials for Hitler's vast architectural schemes. A new SS enterprise was established, the

German Earth and Stone Works, and two new concentration camps, Flossenbürg and Mauthausen, were sited near quarries. The labour was gruelling and the prisoners, mostly designated as recidivist criminals and 'asocials', were treated with sadistic brutality; death rates were correspondingly far higher than in the other pre-war camps. Here was the nucleus of the rapidly expanding conglomerate of SS business enterprises and slave labour forces which, as we will see in Chapter 9, became integrated in the war economy.

SS racial policy

Alongside the security apparatus and the emerging SS economy, the third pillar of SS power was the conduct of racial policy. This was intimately bound up with Himmler's cranky blood-and-soil fixation on the restoration of Germanic 'purity' and his fantasy of the SS as a racial and ideological order destined eventually to colonize and rule a new Teutonic-Nordic empire in the east. While Himmler indulged his obsessions, Heydrich was put in practical charge of SS anti-Jewish policy, and his staff of self-appointed 'experts' made Jewish emigration their top priority. The SD pressed for the 'Jewish question' to be solved not by rabid propaganda and random violence, but by orderly policy-making, public education, and targeted intimidation. They treated Jewish Germans as a security threat, an enemy fifth column that must be forced out of the country before the anticipated war began (see Chapter 5).

The SD had no monopoly in this key area of Nazi ideology and policy, but a crucial turning point came in 1938, which brought the annexations of Austria in March and the Sudetenland in September, and in November the *Kristallnacht* pogrom (see Chapters 5 and 7). The annexations were followed by forced population resettlements that suggested an accelerating time frame for Himmler's dream of an ethnically reorganized Europe, while the pogrom ushered in a regime-wide re-evaluation and intensification of anti-Jewish policy. Himmler accordingly began to claim a more assertive role for the SS. The new Central Office for Jewish Emigration organized in Vienna by the ambitious SS bureaucrat Adolf Eichmann in August 1938 became the model for similar agencies established in Berlin and Prague. Indicatively, the unstable boundary between intensified pressure for emigration and forced deportation was already crossed in October, when Himmler's expulsion of 18,000 Polish Jews prompted the reaction that led to *Kristallnacht*.

By 1939, Himmler had expanded and diversified the SS, adding the SS-Totenkopfverbände to guard the concentration camps, and the militarized troops of the Waffen-SS, whose numbers were to reach almost 600,000 by mid-1944. The invasion of Poland in 1939 finally gave him the opportunity to gather the strands of the SS para-state into a strategic military and imperial enterprise. The new territorial horizons opening in the east offered the SS intermeshed roles in conquest, policing, racial engineering, resettlement and colonization, and, ultimately, genocide, as we will see in Chapters 8 and 9.

Chapter 5
Volksgemeinschaft: Community and exclusion

State power was a necessary but not sufficient condition for the realization of the National Socialist vision of Germany reborn. A cliché of Nazi political theory and propaganda, as we saw in Chapter 4, was that the state was not an end in itself, but a means to an end. That end was the realization of the historic destiny of the German *Volk*, forged into an integral national racial community, or *Volksgemeinschaft*, under Nazi leadership. The term *Volksgemeinschaft* itself was common enough in German political discourse, but what it meant in Nazi Germany specifically has been a matter of considerable debate among historians. This is because it is so closely tied to fundamental questions about the power of Nazi ideology to colonize Germans' beliefs and attitudes, and about the measure of their consent to the violent political and social experiment undertaken in their name.

Understanding *Volksgemeinschaft*

In the age of the nation state it is a commonplace to see the nation or people as a collectivity transcending its individual members and binding them to a higher purpose. Nazi visions of *Volksgemeinschaft* sat within this familiar and appealing framework, in a post-war Germany divided and disoriented by military defeat, social disorder, and economic crisis; but they added new layers of meaning, if not of coherence. They offered an alternative to the international advance of modern consumerist, market models of social integration, with their emphasis on entitlement, exchange, and choice, in favour of a racially selective, militant, and autarkic model of national solidarity. Despite the Nazis' archaic rhetoric of German blood and soil (*Blut und Boden*), this was perhaps not so much an anti-modern vision as an alternative present, with a footing in its own ersatz sciences of racial purity and demographic expansion.

Yet it was not ideological conviction that sold the regime to the German public. Rather, one of the loudest and most repetitive boasts of the Nazi regime after 1933 was that it had created something new and forward-looking: an organic but competitive community (*Leistungsgemeinschaft*) that effaced the oppressive social hierarchies of the past in favour of reward for merit. Those who met new racial and social criteria for membership in the *Volksgemeinschaft* and contributed their due were offered a flattering image of themselves as valued members of this privileged ethnic community. Even the sceptical could be attracted by the regime's seductive promises of community and shared responsibility in a newly self-reliant Germany. These promises included full employment and improved standards of living and welfare, social discipline and family stability, orderly relations between men and women, and life chances secured not by the inequities of wealth and status, but by contests of ability and effort.

Historians have tended to treat these claims sceptically as a propaganda smokescreen with little grounding in lived reality. In this view, the Nazi insistence on the new classlessness ignored the fact that German workers were not integrated in a new national community, but had to be cowed into submission by the violent destruction of their political organizations and workplace freedoms. The endless iterations of *Volksgemeinschaft* were intended to obscure the persistence of ineradicable class differentiations and to disavow the production of new social hierarchies and economic inequalities. They also veiled Hitler's fantasy of world domination through war, for which a solid and reliable home front was indispensable. Behind the fraudulent artifice of *Gleichschaltung*—the coordination of German institutions into a cohesive, Nazified whole—the reality was a splintered population stuck in stagnant inequality. Wealth and property were not redistributed; real hourly wages barely rose; housing construction was sacrificed to rearmament. Power was transferred to new party elites, even as, despite the populist rhetoric, the old bourgeoisie and aristocracy retained much of their status and authority (and their convictions: upper-class German nationalists cultivated a snobbish disdain for the boorish leaders they had helped bring to power). Meanwhile, according to this interpretation, the powerless mass of the people was bribed with empty promises and coerced into acquiescence in a police state, where 'security' was another name for terror and their destiny was war.

Is this picture more realistic than the regime's own claims? It is clear that the Nazi regime's primary objective in 1933 was to suppress effective political opposition by crushing the left; equally, that it left core social inequalities untouched and created new ones, even while attempting to manufacture and enforce an image of popular consent. Yet ideology is not reducible solely to propaganda. Positing 'Nazis' as the authors of prescriptions and policies directed at a passive audience of 'Germans', who could either comply or resist, is over-simple. It does not take enough account of the real textures and experiences of social and private life in a society where familiar paths of collective identity and expression had suddenly been blocked. And our angle of vision has altered as historical research into Nazi Germany has moved from an older concentration on class and the limits of resistance to take more account of racial politics. Questions of identity and belonging in a society defined by new biopolitical classifications, rather than by social categories and political loyalties, have acquired greater prominence. Close attention to the history of everyday life in Nazi Germany has exposed the intricate pathways that insinuated National Socialism—as party, ideology, language, policy—into the lives and identities of Germans of all classes and political backgrounds. Against the freedoms they had lost under National Socialism, millions could choose to selectively disregard the ideology and count what they had gained: jobs in an expanding economy, a reassuring sense of ethnic entitlement, patriotic pride in Germany's military strength and international standing after the 'shame' of Versailles. Hundreds of thousands of fellow Germans were soon to discover that the choice was not theirs to make—but the majority were willing to stomach the price these others paid.

Defining boundaries

The foundation of this community of belonging was first and foremost the forced exclusion of all those deemed unworthy of admission. The Nazi regime was prepared to adopt unprecedentedly radical measures to hammer the mosaic diversity of German society into a weapon forged for demographic growth, racial struggle, and territorial expansion. Inadequate and unwanted people were to be locked behind real and rhetorical barriers that would separate them from the *Volksgemeinschaft* and become impermeable to ordinary sentiments of recognition and empathy.

The bedrock principle of the *Volksgemeinschaft* was therefore to define and police the boundaries between who was fit to belong and who was not. The liberal concepts of 'individual' and 'citizen' were superseded by the biologized category of the *Volksgenosse*. One of many grossly ideological words that took over public discourse after 1933, this has no exact English equivalent but only awkwardly literal translations, such as 'ethnic comrade'. Its core value was not political or civil rights but 'blood' in the sense of biological fitness—the racial and eugenic worth of the *Volksgenosse* for the life and growth of an organic community.

Outside this category were placed all those 'others' from whom the *Volksgemeinschaft* had to be protected and purged, now designated as *artfremd* ('alien to the [racial] type'), *gemeinschaftsfremd* ('alien to the community', or 'asocial'), or *erbkrank* (hereditarily ill). The state would encourage biologically healthy (and politically acceptable) Germans to flourish and reproduce, while eliminating all those whose defects threatened to harm this literal 'body politic'. The tenets and practices of eugenics, or what the Nazis preferred to call racial hygiene, were by no means peculiar to Nazi Germany: they were commonplace in early 20th-century science and social policy in Europe and the USA, and had already made some headway in Germany before 1933. But in Nazi Germany, unrestrained by now silenced critical voices, a radical new consensus and impetus for coercive programmes was forged. Medical ambition converged with officially endorsed racial ideology to treat the challenge of unfitness as an urgent matter of collective biopolitical self-defence. As one Nazi leader put it bluntly in 1934, National Socialism was simply 'applied biology'.

The 'asocial' and criminal

'Asocial' was the catch-all label applied to deviant and insubordinate individuals or groups who were racially 'Aryan' but who, as Heydrich put it in 1938, 'demonstrate through behaviour which is inimical to the community, but which need not be criminal, that they will not adapt themselves to the community'—a dangerously elastic definition. In the same way that the mass detention of political opponents was publicly justified as protecting the community from the threat of Bolshevism, so the incarceration of unpopular deviant and marginal groups was represented not simply as a 'war on crime', but as an equally urgent weapon of national defence against a corrosive social danger.

Enumerated by the Bavarian political police in 1936, the targets were a ragbag of men and women of whom most had long been subject to official harassment: 'Beggars, vagabonds, gypsies, vagrants, work-shy individuals, idlers, prostitutes, grumblers, habitual drunkards, hooligans, traffic offenders, and so-called psychopaths and mental cases'. These were now arrested en masse and thrown into prisons, workhouses, and concentration camps, while new powers of preventive detention exposed tens of thousands of allegedly dangerous 'habitual' and 'hereditary' criminals to the same fate. At first, Sinti and Roma ('Gypsies') were persecuted as vagrants or work-shy, but in 1938 a decree issued by Himmler described them, menacingly, not just as a problem but as an alien race. Between them these groups filled the concentration camps, so that by 1939 political prisoners made up no more than one-third of their 21,000 inmates. Hard labour and harsh discipline held out the faint possibility of 're-education' and reintegration into the community, but for most this was an illusion.

Sex, gender, and reproduction

The 'asocial' and criminal were also particularly vulnerable to other high-priority plans for enhancing the stock and quality of Germany's population. A July 1933 law decreed the compulsory sterilization of all those certified as 'hereditarily ill', spanning a wide range of physical and mental defects from feeble-mindedness and alcoholism to hereditary deafness or blindness. The criteria became more elastic in practice, extending to groups of 'asocials' and a small group of Afro-Germans who were mostly the offspring of German women and French African occupation troops stationed in the post-war Rhineland. By 1939, some 320,000 German women and men had been sterilized, and the policy had been so quickly absorbed into public consciousness that the male procedure even acquired its own ironic nickname—the *Hitlerschnitt*.

The exclusion of the unfit from reproduction was tightly interwoven with policies designed to reverse the decline in the German birth rate since the war, conjuring in Nazi eyes a nightmare of racial suicide. Sterilization was forbidden to genetically 'healthy' men and women, while voluntary abortion, already illegal in Germany, was subjected to harsher enforcement and penalties, and access to birth control hampered. Marriage was increasingly regulated by state-imposed racial and ideological criteria, starting with a selective marriage loan scheme in June 1933. Eligibility was restricted by race, female partners were required to leave paid employment, and the repayment of the loan was reduced for each child born. Under the so-called Nuremberg Laws adopted in 1935, marriage and sexual relations between 'Jews' and 'citizens of German or "kindred" (*artverwandtes*) blood' were forbidden. The same year saw a ban on marriages deemed biologically 'undesirable'. This new insistence on reproduction was also intended to undo the uneven gains of feminism in the 1920s, to subject women to a prescriptive ideology of gender roles, and to enforce motherhood as a duty to the community.

The intensified persecution of homosexual men, spearheaded by Himmler, was prompted partly by the vulgar presumption that they refused their procreative duty to the community. Women's allegedly passive sexuality protected lesbians since they were not considered entirely lost to reproduction, but they too were rendered vulnerable by the fierce moralism of Himmler's rigorously binary model of masculinity and femininity. Intercourse between men had long been criminalized in Germany, but in 1935 the criminal code was extended to cover vaguely defined forms of sexual intimacy between men. Many homosexual men were tried and jailed, but some 15,000 were thrown into concentration camps between 1933 and 1945, to be persecuted by SS guards and fellow prisoners alike and made the victims of botched medical experiments.

The new state-enforced imperatives of racial hygiene rode roughshod over all considerations of individual choice or morality and sanctioned grossly intrusive investigations of individuals' sexual, medical, and family histories, especially for women. Gradual shifts in public values, professional codes, and language sapped resistance and reservations, sheltering the new realities from the criticism they might otherwise have provoked, and enabling the even greater violations of medical ethics that took place after 1939 (see Chapter 9). By imposing dichotomous 'us/them' distinctions, the regime's policies withdrew stigmatized groups from normal social interactions and rendered them defenceless against repression and persecution. Conversely, those on the other side of the line could feel a gratifying sense of superiority that further enhanced the distance between insiders and outsiders, a sentiment that provided perhaps the sturdiest prop of the *Volksgemeinschaft*. Yet the public health and welfare programmes to which 'Aryan' Germans were entitled were simply the other side of the coin. Their provision was conditional on exactly those principles of racial and eugenic discrimination that treated all individuals merely as biological units of the *Volk*.

Jews

Of all those sacrificed to the Nazi vision of *Volksgemeinschaft*, the most relentlessly persecuted were Germany's Jewish citizens. In 1933, Germans who identified as Jews numbered some 503,000, or 0.76 per cent of the population. More than two-thirds lived in the largest cities such as Frankfurt and Berlin, and this yielded a typically urban and bourgeois social profile. Educated Jews were prominent in the professions, finance and commerce, and arts and letters, while men and women further down the social scale earned their living as artisans, shopkeepers, or factory workers. More than a century of formal Jewish emancipation and advances in social integration in the 1920s, including high rates of intermarriage with Christians, had resulted in a highly assimilated community; of the ninety Jews living in the city of Weimar in 1933, for example, a third were married to Christians. Although it is customary to speak of 'the' Jewish community, Jewish Germans were divided by class and religious attitudes. Many old-established families were liberal or secular in their views and liable to disdain the minority of so-called 'Ostjuden'—the often stateless, impoverished, and ultra-observant Jews who had left eastern Europe more recently.

That Jewish Germans of all stripes would be exposed to new extremes of antisemitism was a given in 1933: unclear only was the form and direction this would take. To begin with, the regime was able to draw on antisemitic prejudices widespread in Germany as in the rest of Europe, especially indignation at the supposedly 'disproportionate influence' of Jews in public life. The presence of this allegedly powerful and racially alien group constituted the 'Jewish question' which the Nazis were determined to 'solve' for Germany once and for all. Pending this, the regime's intention was not only to close the track of equality and assimilation, to encourage emigration, and to remove Jews from the paths and pursuits of normal life; it was also to erect impermeable barriers between 'Jew' and 'German'. This was no apartheid state: the architecture of alleged Jewish difference was constructed not to force two communities to coexist in separate spaces, but to prepare for a Germany 'free' of Jews. Yet how this was to be achieved was less the product of a single-minded strategy than the outcome of the competing dynamics and tensions that characterized the exercise of power in Nazi Germany.

But who actually *was* 'Jewish'? This all-important question could not remain solely a matter of vulgar prejudice but required some kind of usable definition. Nazi antisemitism was, like any racism, a congeries of ideology, pseudo-science, and bigotry that did not lend itself to categorical precision or scientific validation. But crucially, the Nazis usurped the prerogative of definition, expropriating Jews' right to claim their own identity: from 1933, this was decided for them in the language of 'blood'. This meant that conversion to Christianity was no protection against being deemed racially Jewish, and that crude physiological criteria were applied to settle dubious cases. Jewish opinion was now irrelevant.

'Non-Aryan' descent based on parents' and grandparents' religion was the criterion chosen for the first racial purge of the civil service in 1933. This 'Aryan clause' was then applied far and wide, as the stain of antisemitic discrimination and persecution seeped into German life, determining everything from what name you could have to whom you could marry, from where you could be educated to what career you could choose, from where you could live to how you could spend your leisure time. These principles also demanded that all non-Jewish Germans had to certify that they were untainted by ancestral Jewish 'blood', spawning a giant new industry of genealogical research (*Sippenforschung*).

A more elaborate and comprehensive regulation came as a result of the Nuremberg Laws, adopted in September 1935 by a special session of the Reichstag held at the Nazi Party's annual rally. The law 'For the Protection of German Blood and German Honour' banned marriage and sexual relations between Jews and 'citizens of German or kindred blood'—the preferred official designation for non-Jews. Together with a new law restricting full citizenship to this group, the regulations legally consigned Jews to second-class status. Supplementary regulations imposed a rather less stringent definition of 'full Jew' (*Volljude*) than hitherto, but also established complicated subcategories, creating tens of thousands of part-Jews, or 'Mischlinge', whose mixed status only blurred the attempted line of demarcation. Exposing the spurious science of 'blood', formal religious affiliation remained the basis of these categorizations.

German Jews' experience after 1933 was determined by a tangled and unpredictable dynamic of grass-roots terror and state-sanctioned persecution, backed by growing social isolation as their fellow Germans withdrew. Although naked violence by Nazi activists attracted some public dismay, ritualized insults and humiliations—parades of placarded Jewish offenders, boycotts that publicly identified Jewish-owned businesses—could be occasions for popular demonstrations affirming the solidarity of the non-Jewish community (Figure 4). Antisemitic propaganda leached into every sphere of life, reshaping the very language in which 'Germans' and 'Jews' were able to think about each other or communicate across racial boundaries. Crude public notices announced 'Jews not welcome here' or 'This town is free of Jews'. The 'Reich Association of German Jews' was obliged to change its name to 'Reich Association of Jews in Germany', and the press was similarly instructed to avoid any language that suggested the existence of 'German Jews'. Jews were segregated on paper in census entries and residential records. From January 1938 their separate status was documented in obligatory identity cards identifying the holder as Jewish, and their passports were stamped with a prominent letter 'J'.

These strategies aimed to make German Jews visible *only* as 'Jews', and to persuade Germans to recognize them not as individuals but as *der Jude*, the Jew, and literally a race apart. For Jews themselves, this demolition of their own subjective and unquestioned identity as German was deeply insulting and painful. 'Whatever may happen politically, inwardly I am definitively changed,' wrote Victor Klemperer, an assimilated Jewish academic and decorated veteran, in October 1938. 'No one can take my Germanness away from me, but my nationalism and patriotism are gone forever.'

By the later 1930s, Jewish Germans had been evicted from schools and universities and their cultural works purged from stage and concert repertoires, libraries, and art galleries. Antisemitic research into the history and racial character of 'the Jew' acquired academic respectability. Jews were forced out of employment and the professions, and excluded from public services. Their businesses were boycotted and driven to bankruptcy; the fiscal authorities colluded in the forcible 'Aryanization' of their property, squeezed Jewish taxpayers to the hilt, and steered the proceeds into the rearmament drive.

4. SA men install an antisemitic placard on a road into Weimar in August 1935. The photograph was captioned: 'German mothers! Keep your sheltering hand over your child! Protect him from the Jews!'

Jewish Germans were shunned and betrayed by erstwhile friends and colleagues, and exposed to unpredictable assaults on their freedom and self-respect. They were driven from clubs and societies and banned from cinemas, parks, swimming pools, and other facilities. Most responded to this bewildering onslaught by drawing more closely together: geographically, as they abandoned smaller communities to seek the greater anonymity of big cities, and socially, as they sought security within the family, the synagogue, and the new self-help organizations.

Pressure for Jews to emigrate, a policy spearheaded by Heydrich's SD, was intense, although it was simultaneously hindered by their systematic impoverishment. Jewish Germans faced agonizing decisions about whether to uproot themselves from their homeland, sever family ties, relinquish their property to the state, and start life again in some unfamiliar and probably unwelcoming country. Those seeking to leave encountered closed borders at every turn; by the end of 1937, to the frustration of policy-makers and Nazi activists alike, only about a quarter of the Jewish population had left Germany. Hitler vented his fury at this situation in a ferociously antisemitic speech at the party's 1937 Nuremberg rally, which prompted new antisemitic outrages by local activists and further discriminatory measures intended to force Jews out of their remaining niches in economic life. As the regime ratcheted up its preparations for war, evicting the Jewish 'fifth column' from German life became an urgent priority. The shocking violence and radically intensified persecution in annexed Austria after March 1938 and anti-Jewish riots in major German cities prompted renewed numbers to flee—but, for the regime, still too few. It was at this impasse that anti-Jewish policy took a lurch forward from which there was to be no return.

On 7 November 1938, a German embassy official was shot in Paris by a young Jew, Herschel Grynszpan, whose parents were among thousands of stateless 'Ostjuden' expelled into Poland at the end of October. The assassination was seized by Goebbels as an opportunity to take leadership of grassroots Nazi discontent with the slow pace of anti-Jewish action in Germany, by contrast with its more radical progress in annexed Austria. With Hitler's approval, Goebbels and senior Nazi officials orchestrated a pogrom across Germany on the night of 9/10 November, while publicly proclaiming that this was a spontaneous act of popular revenge for a Jewish crime.

The harrowing violence that now engulfed Germany's Jews was carried out by SA and SS men wearing civilian clothes, egged on by specially summoned party members and witnessed by crowds, some of whom joined in, while the police stood by. This so-called 'Night of the Broken Glass' (*Kristallnacht*) exceeded anything hitherto. In a terrifying escalation of violence, a thousand synagogues in Germany were desecrated and demolished; thousands of Jewish-owned shops and businesses were smashed up and looted, homes invaded and plundered, men and women brutally assaulted. In Weimar, the last Jewish-owned shop, a small stationer's, was ransacked by SA and SS men and its proprietor, an elderly woman, manhandled. At least ninety-one people were killed across Germany and unknown numbers committed suicide. Some 26,000 Jewish men, including twelve from Weimar, were thrown into overcrowded concentration camps where hundreds more soon died. An inmate of Buchenwald described their arrival: 'Jews by the dozen, by the carload, by the hundred and by the thousand. In all stages of life—wounded, sick, crippled, with broken limbs, missing eyes, fractured skulls, half dead, and dead'. Those who survived could be released only with proof that they had procured valid emigration papers.

The reaction of those who had not participated was subdued. Many non-Jewish Germans were shocked and even shamed by the scale of the violence and the wanton destruction of property, but few were willing to intervene: a gauge not only of fear but of the reach of antisemitic sentiments and the success with which Jews had been isolated. Among Nazi leaders, Goebbels's rabble-rousing initiative was not seen as entirely constructive, but it released new antisemitic energy in the regime, and was followed by a raft of draconian measures that attempted to systematize the relationship between policies of persecution, expropriation, and emigration. Göring, a bitter critic of the disorder and destruction, was now entrusted by Hitler with coordinating the regime's anti-Jewish policies. Yet a fundamental contradiction remained: while Göring's priority of seizing Jewish assets for his economic programme lay within the regime's control, Heydrich's goal of mass emigration, despite an upsurge in numbers, did not. Whether through frustration or in an attempt to blackmail foreign governments, Hitler and other Nazi spokesmen now began to utter even more explicit threats against Jews if they remained in Germany. At the same time, propaganda increasingly projected the *Volksgemeinschaft* as a vital community of self-defence against a global Jewish enemy bent on Germany's destruction.

Chapter 6
Volksgemeinschaft: Control and belonging

Understanding how Germans were involved with the National Socialist regime involves not only measuring support or opposition on a binary scale, but also tracing the overlapping patterns of enthusiasm, satisfaction, indifference, and aversion that were woven into people's lives and sense of self. In everyday life, Germans who were neither categorically excluded from the community, nor enthusiastic supporters of Nazism, faced an often mundane repertoire of experiences and decisions about how to conduct themselves and how to gauge the boundaries between identification, compliance, and infraction: whether to join the Nazi Party, fly a swastika flag, protest against the removal of crucifixes from a Catholic school, greet a Jewish acquaintance on the street, denounce a neighbour to the authorities. People's behaviour might endorse Nazi expectations in one context but evade or repudiate them in another, yielding a muddier but more realistic picture of the relationships between the regime and its subjects.

The promise of *Volksgemeinschaft* may ultimately have been hollow, but for Germans who met its criteria, especially young people, it opened new horizons of opportunity, belonging, and recognition. For ambitious men (and some women) from modest backgrounds who endorsed or could tolerate the new racial values, Nazi Germany offered rewarding careers and status in the new elites—the ballooning party and police bureaucracies, the new managerial and technocratic specialists of the booming arms economy, the vastly expanded armed forces. Because a good deal of what the NSDAP peddled as its own communitarian ideal was actually a repackaging of far more widespread sentiments, familiarity allowed many Germans to identify with what they recognized while discounting the regime's more noxious tendencies. These insights can help us to understand not only how Germans were supposed to lead their lives under National Socialism, but how they actually did.

The bid to establish this German community was heavily underwritten by Germany's rapid economic recovery since January 1933, when Hitler had demanded 'four years' to tackle the crisis and the sharpened social conflicts it had brought. Even if the Nazis stole the credit for an economic upturn that had already begun shortly before they took power, this recovery was crucial in stabilizing and embedding the government. The decline in unemployment, achieved through programmes of work creation and rearmament, was probably the single most important factor in blunting the edge of working-class hostility to the Nazi regime, although intense workplace discipline and a stagnant standard of living continued to provoke powerful resentments on the shop floor. Economic recovery promised a return to normality for the urban and rural middle classes too, reopening blocked opportunities, raising incomes and consumption, and helping to banish fears of Bolshevism and class war. The ubiquitous promotion of hard-won unity and stabilization after years of division and crisis was crucial in legitimizing Hitler's dictatorship as the indispensable guarantee of strong leadership and national discipline.

At the same time, legitimacy had limited meaning in a society unable to openly discuss the chasm between what the regime claimed, and what it actually would or could deliver. Nazi leaders faced a complex balancing act between the interests of competing social constituencies—workers and employers, big industrialists and small businesses, agrarian landlords and peasant smallholders—and these conflicts did not simply vanish when the Nazi Party proclaimed its new era of national unity. The regime also had to juggle ambitious economic objectives that were determined by the overriding imperative of preparing Germany for war. And it had to try to veil the resultant tensions: the massively uneven distribution of the fruits of economic recovery, and the economic distortions generated by the forced pace of rearmament, which threatened more than once to topple the whole shaky edifice.

The situation of women, so pivotal to the regime's demographic and social priorities, illustrates the scope of these contradictions. The Nazi cult of domesticity and motherhood found wide approval among women as well as men, yet this ideology and the policies encouraging high birth rates were hard to reconcile with the growing need to tap women's labour when shortages became critical after 1937. Attempts to foster family farms, a key priority of Nazi 'blood and soil' ideology, not only faltered, but as men abandoned agriculture for more lucrative industrial employment women were left to shoulder the burdens of farm work. Policies to deter middle-class women from university education and the professions were similarly confounded by the increasing demand for trained professional labour. In a mockery of the ideology of *Volksgemeinschaft*, middle-class girls also found it easy to evade the year of 'voluntary' labour service: a class privilege massively resented by those who did not share it.

Limits of opposition

The regime itself was well aware of such problems, but for others to draw attention to them was fraught with risk, while organized opposition or resistance that intended to damage the regime was crushed wherever it emerged. Even though most Germans did not experience this directly, Nazi Germany remained a police state backed by terror and violence. With the silencing of pluralist voices and the dissolution of familiar underpinnings of independent social life, even reluctant Germans could learn to collude in their own de facto integration. Most political activists eventually resigned themselves to waiting for liberation by defeat in the war they knew was coming; they concentrated on preserving skeletons of their organizational networks for a post-Nazi future. Where collective life was not corroded by fear, it was liable to be compromised by distrust. Familiar milieux—the workplace, the pub, even the family—became unreliable. The tangle of trade unions, voluntary associations, and local clubs hitherto braided into German social life was now destroyed or 'coordinated', or else dwindled and died.

The only surviving institutions that offered some semblance of an alternative ideology and identity were the Protestant and Catholic churches; but their independence was compromised, especially in the case of Protestants, by their enthusiasm for Nazism as a shield against godless Marxism and materialism. Given that 95 per cent of Germans were formally members of one or other of the two denominations, regime propaganda was equally keen to exploit the authority of Christian values, even if this did not entirely silence more anti-Christian and anticlerical ideologues in the SS. Dealing with open religious resistance was another matter. Jehovah's Witnesses suffered unremitting persecution for their dogmatic refusal to bow to the state in any way. The establishment of an antisemitic 'German Christian' church that repudiated the Old Testament led to the secession of orthodox Protestant 'confessing Christians', some of whom, like individual Catholic priests, were willing to confront the regime and face the consequences. Otherwise, the church hierarchies largely focused on protecting their own institutional existence; Jews could look for succour only if they were baptized or in mixed marriages. In the rest of society, resistance was confined to small numbers of courageous individuals and precarious groups and networks motivated by political or ethical convictions. Their actions, repeatedly overwhelmed by Gestapo repression, included workplace sabotage, disseminating illegal literature, protecting individuals at risk, and maintaining contact with the wartime Allies. Other Germans simply endeavoured to preserve the habit of independent thought through what came to be called 'inner emigration': a withdrawal into private worlds of belief and morality.

The Nazi party in control

The vast majority of *Volksgenossen*—in attitudes ranging from enthusiastic embrace to tight-lipped silence—reconciled or resigned themselves to a Germany now controlled by the NSDAP. The party was supposed to be the great engine of *Volksgemeinschaft*, powering a revolution of values as well as social structures that would leave neither private relations nor social networks untouched. By 1939, eight million Germans, or 10 per cent of the population, were members of the party (*Parteigenossen*) organized at the grass roots by 250,000 cell and block leaders. Tens of millions more were members of one or more of the plethora of official Nazi organizations, including the SA or SS, and the Hitler Youth or League of German Girls—these a supreme priority for a regime intent on indoctrinating the next generation. What these memberships actually meant in terms of ideological conviction was uneven.

Other arms of the Nazi colossus took over labour, welfare, sports, and organized leisure, and managed occupational and social groups from teachers and doctors to veterans and women. The Deutsche Arbeitsfront (DAF), the mass-membership labour organization led by the erratic Robert Ley and charged with the crucial task of controlling the working class, employed 44,000 paid and 1.3 million unpaid officials. Its most popular sections, Beauty of Labour (SdA) and Strength Through Joy (KdF), provided workplace amenities, organized leisure, and subsidized holidays for the masses; it organized the travel of 10,000 football fans to London for a December 1935 friendly at White Hart Lane, and built a 'KdF town' in Berlin to receive German visitors to the 1936 Olympics. Run from the top down by the strictly hierarchical

Führerprinzip, these gigantic monopolies were supposed to combine popular mobilization with political surveillance, as officials used their positions to monitor local morale and report on suspect persons or activities.

The highpoints of the party's annual calendar—the Nuremberg rallies, the Winter Relief charity campaign (Figure 5)—communicated loud messages of national unity. Other events promoted by party officials latched on to traditional rituals and iconographies of identity and community, from harvest festivals to Christmas, as well as mounting cultural and sporting activities to celebrate local histories and loyalties. Nationally, the labour movement's May Day festival was supplanted by a statutory 'Day of National Labour' organized by the DAF. *Volkstrauertag,* the national day of mourning for the war dead instituted in 1926, became *Heldengedenktag* (Heroes' Memorial Day), a nationalistic and cultish celebration of sacrificial death from which the churches were excluded.

The vainest ambitions of the 'Third Reich' were embodied in the scale and putative durability of architecture, town planning, and roads. Its road-building programme was intended not just for military use, but for the no less political purpose of tourism: to enable Germans to appreciate, through Nazi eyes, the natural and cultural heritage of their fatherland. Led by Hitler's grandiose plans for the reconstruction of Berlin, the regime proposed to transform every Gau capital into an architectural incarnation of the new Reich, with monumental neoclassical party buildings and vernacular housing developments. Street names were updated to commemorate Nazi heroes such as Horst Wessel, and numerous towns and cities found space for an Adolf-Hitler-Platz. Streetscapes were also transformed by the party's visual propaganda—not only the mass displays of swastika bunting marking special occasions, but the drumbeat of hortatory posters and hoardings that competed with commercial advertising and kept the Nazi Party and its campaigns in the public eye.

5. Poster for the annual Winter Relief Campaign. The swastika shares the space with traditional winter imagery and the text 'Think of Christmas, donate to the 1933/34 Winter Relief Campaign of the German People for the battle against hunger and cold'.

The propaganda ministry made extensive efforts to control the media and communications and to insulate Germany from international culture. Writers and artists were licensed by state-run chambers of culture which excluded Jews and the politically suspect and rebooted the careers of third-rate political hacks. Museums and galleries were eventually stripped of thousands of works of 'degenerate' modernist art, while theatrical and musical performances were restricted to approved repertoires purged of 'degenerate' works—no more Mendelssohn in the concert hall, although churches still contrived to play his religious compositions anonymously. Books by unacceptable authors, from Heinrich Heine to Bertolt Brecht, were publicly burned and purged from libraries and schools. As intellectuals too were purged, and university curricula from anthropology to zoology invaded by Nazi values, a mass exodus of Jewish and dissident scholars and scientists dispersed some of Germany's finest minds across the world. A shrinking number of nominally independent newspapers and magazines survived, with their journalists forced to toe the party line. They faced the competition of the subsidized Nazi press, which commanded 85 per cent of the market by 1945. The foreign press was regularly reviled by Goebbels as a 'factory of lies' (*Lügenfabrik*). Radio and the cinema were effective party monopolies, 'Negro' jazz was banned, Hollywood denigrated and German film-making fostered, and commercial advertising subjected to intrusive political controls.

In Weimar, where Schiller's 175th birthday was ostentatiously celebrated in 1934, the poet was commandeered as a nationalist and racist. There too Gauleiter Sauckel, having temporarily hijacked a wing of the main museum as his headquarters, pursued his vision of transforming sleepy Thuringia into Germany's 'Green Heart', a national magnet of culture, tourism, and economic enterprise. Plans for a vast new 'Gau Forum' in the central Karl-August-Platz (inevitably renamed Platz Adolf Hitlers) were initiated in July 1936 with a groundbreaking ceremony performed by the Führer himself. It was never completed, and was fated to be popularly ridiculed as the 'Sauckropolis'.

Everyday life

The noise of propaganda bequeathed to history suggests that life in Nazi Germany was entirely orchestrated by the Nazi Party and always lived collectively at top political volume. Victor Klemperer derided the ceaseless round of party activity and what he called 'the curse of the superlative'—every public event 'historic' and 'unique', every achievement 'total' and 'eternal'. But, as Goebbels understood, propaganda was as much about communication and entertainment as ideological dictation. The regime could accumulate political capital more securely not by naked propaganda, but by shrouding its political messages in more palatable packaging through media such as romantic films and radio request programmes. In any case, attempts to control culture and communications could never be total, nor could audience responses be assumed. In practice people embraced whatever they approved, ignored whatever they disliked, and left active participation to the convinced party faithful.

Germans' lives were also negotiated on a more mundane plane, in microcosmic or oblique everyday situations that straddled the frontier between the public and the private, the collective and the individual, obligation and choice. Undramatic in themselves, these situations remind us that the regime's objective was less to impose a rigid ideological orthodoxy than to redefine automatic habits of thought and behaviour, and engender a new National Socialist sense of self.

The Hitler greeting

The *Deutsche Gruss* or *Hitlergruss*—the stiff raised-arm gesture, the staccato 'Heil Hitler!'—had become familiar in Germany since the Nazi Party made it compulsory for its members in 1926. After 1933, the gesture and words were hammered into public consciousness not only by the set-piece highlights of Nazi public ceremony, but also by a sudden and more pervasive change in social conventions. Using the *Hitlergruss* was only made legally obligatory in specific circumstances—in the presence of the flag, for example, or by public officials—but it quickly infiltrated social life. The greeting was understood to declare one's political allegiance to the Führer as a *Volksgenosse* (Jews were forbidden to use it), and failure to employ it in ordinary social encounters communicated a message of dissociation from the regime's expectations, if not necessarily of opposition.

The impact of the *Hitlergruss* on social relations was insidious. This uniform and rigid formula competed with a rich repertoire of existing conventions and regional greetings—*Grüss Gott, Servus, Jo, Moin-Moin*—and dislodged gestures such as the handshake or the raised hat through which degrees of acquaintanceship or deference were mutually acknowledged. It made each act of social civility into a political performance that automatically pinned Germans in the embrace of *Volksgemeinschaft*. People knew it was risky to refuse it, even though their behaviour was policed more by anxiety than sanction. One of Klemperer's fellow-academics in Dresden described the tentative gavotte danced as colleagues entered his office in 1934. They arrived 'first with their arm stretched out, Hitler salute. Then they feel their way into the conversation. Then, when they've become certain, the mask falls. I too have to raise my arm. I say "Heil"—but I cannot utter "Heil Hitler".'

Names

Names are keys to personal identity, not only in public but in the intimate way they bind individuals to family and a sense of self. German states had long claimed the right to regulate personal names, and the adoption of fixed surnames by Jews in the course of their 19th-century emancipation was disfigured by the antisemitic prejudice that they should not be allowed to 'hide' their Jewish identity behind a 'German' surname. Under the Nazi regime, the fault-line between 'German' and 'Jewish' names became officially impermeable. In August 1938, as part of a tightening of identification requirements, Jewish Germans were restricted to a list of approved 'Jewish' forenames, vetted by Hitler himself and selected from the most traditional Yiddish stock. The great majority who did not already bear one of them now had to add a new compulsory name—'Sara' or 'Israel'—to their entries in the civil registers. Very few had the opportunity or stubbornness that allowed one Berlin teacher, Dora Lux, to avoid inflicting this humiliating new identity on herself—a decision that kept her 'race' invisible to the authorities and ultimately helped her to survive.

Non-Jews experienced no comparable degree of interference in their personal names, although this did not mean they were entirely free to choose. Attempts to give girls feminized versions of Hitler's name (Hitlerike, Hitlerine) were numerous enough to prompt an official ban in July 1933. Civil register offices were instructed in 1937 that German children should be given only German names; but because no prescriptive list was ever issued, officials were launched into time-consuming researches into historical etymology. Some parents were willing to test this leeway to the hilt, as in a dogged but unsuccessful struggle by a Protestant pastor, starting in 1938, to name his daughter Esther. An opposite kind of dissatisfaction was voiced by non-Jewish Germans petitioning to change a surname that, by sounding 'Jewish', damaged their reputation. The authorities generally looked favourably on these requests.

Clothes

Not everyone in Nazi Germany wore a uniform and leather boots. This may be obvious, but it is a reminder that clothing and appearance were arenas in which individual desires, commercial interests, and regime priorities and expectations had to coexist—especially for women. National Socialism was hardly unique in insisting on allegedly 'traditional' gender roles and the subordination of women to motherhood and the patriarchal family, and dress epitomized the tension between traditional and modernizing impulses in Nazi Germany. The regime's ideological priorities met a generation of women familiar with an emergent consumer economy, to whom film stars and commercial advertising offered seductive images of fashion and cosmetic beauty. Nazi ideology repudiated allegedly alien 'American' or 'Jewish' influences on popular consumption: these symbolized the febrile materialist individualism of urban, commercial modernity that was supposedly the opposite of the authentic German values embodied in the *Volksgemeinschaft*. But while 'beauty' was now to be detached from surface appearance and accorded a new racial value, the messages at work in Nazi Germany were by no means consistent.

Nazi women's organizations pushed *Tracht*, the traditional rural women's garb of blouse, bodice, apron, and dirndl skirt, ideally all home-made by farm women. Not surprisingly, this impractical and time-consuming style did not become more popular with farmers wives, but instead the 'peasant look' was taken over as a fashion style and an explicit expression of support for National Socialism (Figure 6). More widely propagated was the more adaptable ideal of the 'natural' beauty of tanned, physically fit, and loosely clad female bodies, uncontaminated by lipstick or plucked eyebrows. This image was useful not only to the champions of reproductive racial health but also to commercial magazines, which could plug the products of the fashion and cosmetics industries as 'natural' and 'discreet', and let their readers close their ears to the barrage of counter-propaganda.

Laughter

Humour was not banned in Nazi Germany, even if laughing out loud in the wrong place could get you into trouble. Unofficial

6. Austrian women clad in 'traditional' dirndl outfits stand among crowds greeting Hitler on his official visit to Vienna after the *Anschluss* in March 1938.

humour in repressive societies carries a whiff of subversion, but Orwell's claim that 'Every joke is a tiny revolution' goes too far. It is at least as likely that jokes allow both teller and audience to release their frustrations, acting more to reconcile than alienate. This was surely the case with the humour that was directed against the 'Bonzen', the Nazi big shots, whose misconduct fed popular cynicism. Nazi Party cadres cultivated the vices of monopoly power—corruption, arrogance, cronyism, incompetence—on an industrial scale, ridiculing the party's pretensions to iron discipline and dedicated service. Sly jokes mocked their venality—'What is a reactionary? Someone who occupies a position that a Nazi wants'—and suggested novel interpretations of political acronyms: NSDAP, *Na, suchst du auch Pöstchen?* (So you're on the make too?). Joking and injudicious remarks in public could attract serious penalties under a capacious law of October 1934 against 'treacherous attacks on state and party' (the *Heimtückegesetz*); but unless there were additional grounds for suspicion, the Gestapo might choose only to intimidate a first-time offender with an interrogation, followed by a warning or fine. Protection might even arrive from unexpected sources. In October 1935, a court in Weimar dismissed a case on the grounds that the defendant's calling Göring 'a miserable dog' carried a rugged note of approval in Thuringian parlance that had escaped the Sudeten German who denounced him.

Conclusion

Ideologically and institutionally, the claims of *Volksgemeinschaft* ran far beyond their realization. Economic power was not redistributed, class distinctions did not vanish, a 'traditional' gender order was not re-established, Germans did not all become Nazis. It is possible to overestimate the political grasp of the regime, and to miss the more subtle ways in which *Volksgenossen* became complicit in their own identification with it, yet also found opportunities to sidestep this. Whether by choice or anxiety, Germans in the Third Reich not only suspended or disguised old habits and daily behaviours, but also rethought and renegotiated their paths of identity and connection.

Many Germans were willing participants in the Nazi project, gratified by the new opportunities for acting on racist beliefs that had been repressed in the despised republic. The majority who were not active believers in Nazi ideology were able to ease their consent to a racialized *Volksgemeinschaft* through their own more conventional prejudices against Jews and social outsiders. Others again fell into a depoliticized indifference, equally distant from commitment or resistance, and far from the kind of racially enlightened mobilization to which the regime aspired. Many who went their own way without actively endangering the regime were left unmolested; but those who chose to openly reject or courageously resist it risked persecution, and withdrew into small, isolated, and vulnerable groups. For most Germans, it was better to seize such opportunities as were offered, or to grumble and compromise, than to take the risk of critical speech or action, let alone engage in more deliberate opposition. But compromise was the corrosive acid that ate into integrity, and eventually ratified the distinction between insiders and outsiders in the most catastrophic way imaginable.

Chapter 7
Preparing for war

Hitler, National Socialism, and war

The war that Hitler unleashed with the invasion of Poland on
1 September 1939 came as a consummation that the Führer had
sought since 1933 and that other European powers had hoped
to avoid. This was profoundly Hitler's war, but it was also the
ultimate rationale of National Socialism, an ideology in thrall to
fantasies of mastery or immolation. It was Germany's war too,
implicating the German people in conquest, empire-building, and
genocide, to the ultimate disgrace of their country and themselves.

War in the military sense, *Krieg*, shared the Nazi lexicon with
another term, *Kampf*, battle or struggle—a word freighted with
muscular values of masculine comradeship and indomitable
will that were not confined to the military battlefield. It was
sacralized in the title of Hitler's *Mein Kampf* and it saturated Nazi
imagery. The movement's rise to power was the *Kampfzeit*, the
time of struggle; its veteran members were *alte Kämpfer*, old
fighters; and Goebbels titled his 1934 political memoir *Kampf um
Berlin*. After 1933, the public stage was taken over by 'battles' and
'struggles' and 'campaigns' for everything from unemployment to
the harvest. These combative metaphors promoted the core
values of National Socialism, anticipating the goal of the war
itself: not just *Sieg*, but *Endsieg*, final victory.

For Hitler, war was not simply a rational vehicle of policy but also an incarnation of his own and Germany's destiny. This mythic belief justified the extraordinary risks he repeatedly took, to the frequent dismay of his generals and his own entourage. Yet it stood in some tension with the more prosaic lesson he had drawn from the First World War: the need for Germany to avoid the exhausting general war and military stalemate that had supposedly allowed internal enemies to whip mass discontent into revolution in 1918. Hitler spurned the advice of military planners committed to mass mobilization and total war. His strategy was to spare the home front by mounting limited but decisive campaigns that would forestall threats of domestic unrest while delivering epic victories.

Lebensraum and New Order

This oscillation between the metaphysical and the instrumental played out on a monumental double screen: on one side, the bid to open up a vast but ill-defined colonial 'living space' (*Lebensraum*) in the east where the German people could flourish and expand and fulfil its own racial destiny; and, on the other, the idea of establishing a pan-European New Order rescued from Bolshevism, plutocracy, democracy, and international Judaism. As so often, these barely compatible aspirations were not the sole property of the Nazis but were rooted in ideas long cultivated by German nationalists. But in the hands of Hitler and Nazi ideologists such as Himmler, Goebbels, or the agricultural expert Walther Darré, their meaning was to be inflated to the point of racial and geopolitical hyperbole, exploding more conventional understandings of national security, empire, or European reinvention.

Hitler's own sense of what was practically possible shifted according to opportunity and provocation. He had neither a fixed foreign policy calendar nor a blueprint for war and conquest, and he juggled an almost eschatological sense of time with the more banal political calculus of years and decades. If there was a logic at work, it was that every political and military success helped to concretize his goals, to swell his ambitions, to bolster his belief in his own destiny as German history's supreme leader and to convince his satraps of this. By contrast, obstacles and defeats unnerved him, throwing him into a self-indulgent search for scapegoats and sapping his capacity to make clear decisions. This volatile logic also made the course of policy and war acutely vulnerable to the dynamic instability that was intrinsic to power relations in the Nazi regime. Nowhere was this to be more lethal than in the radicalization of Nazi occupation policies during the war. If a kind of productive precarity powered the restless political and military momentum of the Third Reich, it also dictated its ultimate and catastrophic ruin.

Rearmament

Rearmament made a decisive contribution to the recovery of Germany's shattered economy, but also increasingly diverted it towards preparations for war which played havoc with its stability. Its growth began in secret as soon as the Nazis took over existing plans for public spending, but until 1936 it remained relatively modest in scale, concentrating on the expansion of the Wehrmacht (armed forces), the development of an air force, and, in March 1935, the reintroduction of military conscription: all in violation of Versailles. German industrialists and economic experts, as well as the Nazis' conservative allies, welcomed a managed programme of rearmament in itself and as a stepping stone to the recovery of capitalism, the international economy, and the market. But this was not the stance of the Nazi leadership. Their goal was to prepare Germany for aggressive war and to subordinate the German economy to this political priority. This meant giving primacy to rearmament in fiscal policy and the allocation of raw materials; imposing wage and price controls; and attempting to insulate the economy from dependence on imports. Disquiet among industrialists and economists at this wrenching of conventional capitalist perspectives was sharpened in the mid-1930s, when even the ingenuity of the regime's economic expert Hjalmar Schacht could not prevent currency crises, severe threats of inflation, and shortages of essential raw materials and consumer goods that endangered not just rearmament but the economy itself.

The showdown that imposed the primacy of the regime's political objectives and methods was staged in 1936, when Hitler shifted authority over rearmament away from the economic and military leaderships to the Nazi inner circle. The German state was brought directly into industrial production for military purposes, presaging the wartime extension of state ownership and private–public collaborations in occupied Europe. Göring was appointed to direct a new 'Four Year Plan', which was designed to achieve self-sufficiency in strategic raw materials and to establish the economic infrastructure for war. Yet far from resolving the underlying economic tensions, the pace of production and procurement could never satisfy the simultaneous clamour of all parties. Arms production was sustained only by ad hoc strategies that teetered on the brink of crisis and accelerated the need for war to conquer fresh resources. And as their scope became known, these programmes also provoked a European arms race that threatened to leapfrog Germany's own achievements and expose their considerable limitations.

By 1938, rearmament accounted for a colossal 58 per cent of the German budget or 23 per cent of GDP (it had been 1 per cent in 1933). This was now effectively an unprecedented war economy in peacetime, dependent for growth on state procurement. By the time the war began in 1939, the conscript army had been expanded to four million men, and the Luftwaffe, built from scratch, could muster over 4,000 combat aircraft. Civilian work was projected as an equivalent national duty. A gigantic new fortification, the West Wall, was constructed by youthful battalions of the Labour Service (Reichsarbeitsdienst) and the Organisation

Todt to protect Germany's western frontiers. Only naval construction lagged behind. This massive reallocation of national expenditures was largely financed not by adding to already high levels of taxation, but by a growing mountain of public debt. As full employment was reached in 1937, shortages of labour added to the difficulty of maintaining the pace. At the same time, increased state interventions in the economy and constraints on market freedoms were reluctantly accepted by German manufacturers in return for attractive prizes: lucrative state contracts, state-enforced shop-floor discipline, and lavish profits. Here were the first steps into a devil's bargain that would see firms such as IG Farben and Siemens sink deep into complicity with Nazi war crimes.

From rearmament to war, 1933–1939

German rearmament toppled a balance of international relations already troubled by the increasingly brittle post-war settlement. Since the mid-1920s, the post-war distinction between victors and defeated had yielded to an emergent European collective security system; but the 1930s brought a new and unstable distribution of ideological commitments and political alignments among democratic, communist, and fascist powers and their peoples. The financial crisis and the Depression were shaking the political as well as economic foundations of capitalism across Europe and the USA, making the appeal of both fascism and communism freshly acute.

Nazi rhetoric was characteristically bellicose, yet in 1933 Hitler began by projecting himself as a man of peace, a conventional nationalist politician simply representing his state's interests. He could also present a rearmed Germany as a bastion of stability and a bulwark against Bolshevism, the natural ally of any nervous capitalist democracy. In the climate of protectionism and retreat to national sources of security that swayed governmental policies in the 1930s, the Nazis' reassertion of Germany's own political and economic interests and their complaints about 'encirclement' by hostile alliances could appear almost legitimate. Even the regime's insistence on dismissing the remaining constraints on its sovereignty, its noisy demands on behalf of German-speaking minorities in Czechoslovakia and Poland, and its calls for gathering all ethnic Germans 'home into the Reich' might just be interpreted in the League of Nations' sacred languages of national self-determination and minority rights.

For Hitler, these claims served to mask geopolitical objectives that could not be achieved without war; but unless Germany's defences were strengthened and the western powers kept at bay, the climactic campaign of territorial conquest in Russia would carry too many risks. His ideal would therefore be not so much a singular 'war', but a sequence of localized and carefully calibrated political and military victories which would also minimize the strain on the overstretched German arms economy and the home front. In each of these conflicts, Hitler would achieve a preparatory strategic objective or overcome one of his intermediate antagonists without risking a more general war. Germany would then be secure enough to strike out for its ultimate prize of *Lebensraum* in the east.

In the real world of defensive alliances and diplomatic expediency, this strategy encountered a cluster of political and military imponderables which Hitler could sometimes exploit but could not control. His diplomatic priority was to dismantle the interlocking relationships that Germany confronted east and west, which included Germany's own multilateral commitments; regional security pacts in central Europe; France's alliances in the region, notably its 1936 pact with the Soviet Union; and the flagging alignment of France, Britain, and Italy. Germany also needed aggressive economic diplomacy to secure a dominant position in eastern Europe and the Balkans. And Germany needed allies of its own. Despite some serious frictions, a linchpin Rome–Berlin alignment or 'Axis' was negotiated in 1935; it formed the nucleus of the 'Pact of Steel' sealed in May 1939 and the wartime tripartite alliance with Japan.

By the end of 1937, Hitler could chalk up considerable other achievements which disarmed his critics and made him hugely popular within Germany. A spectacularly successful plebiscite returned the industrial Saar region to German control in January 1935, after fifteen years under League administration. The remilitarization (military reoccupation) of the Rhineland in March 1936 was a sensational coup that restored this sensitive region to full German sovereignty, and exposed the inadequacy of the international response at a time when a still weak Germany might have been faced down. But the greater security of the Nazi regime by 1937/8 was accompanied not by stabilization, but by a release from restraints that drove Hitler on to more aggressive postures in his core priorities of foreign policy, military planning, and racial politics.

One key event can stand as an example here. At a secret meeting of top military chiefs called in November 1937 to discuss the worsening shortages of raw materials for rearmament (known as the Hossbach conference), Hitler shocked his audience by tearing the veil off hitherto defensive military planning, and presenting an unexpected and unnerving exposition of his aggressive strategy for *Lebensraum*. He outlined the preparations for its conquest that had to be engaged before Germany lost its competitive edge in the arms race, starting with the destruction of Czechoslovakia, which would bring crucial political, economic, and strategic advantages. Once France and Britain had then been forced into submission, Germany would be free to return to its primary project of eastern conquest.

Those who voiced reservations at these enormously risky calculations—including the war minister Werner von Blomberg, the Wehrmacht commander-in-chief Werner von Fritsch, and the foreign minister Konstantin von Neurath—were soon swept aside in a purge intended to cow dissent. Each discarded general or minister was replaced by a more pliant Nazi appointee, structures of policy-making and command were reorganized, and, in a flight to the centre typical of the regime's crises, Hitler assumed personal command of the Wehrmacht.

From annexation to war, 1938–1940

Under the pressure of Hitler's sense of urgency, events moved rapidly after 1938, as the western democracies were forced into an increasingly reactive posture that swung between conciliation and confrontation. Germany's long-planned annexation of Austria was staged on 12 March 1938 when columns of Wehrmacht troops marched theatrically across the border, to be greeted by cheering crowds and vicious assaults on Jews. In the plebiscite that followed, 98 per cent of voters agreed to sacrifice their independence to *Anschluss* (union) with Germany, ratifying many western Europeans' belief that even this precision-engineered act of ostensible self-determination was not worth a war.

The *Anschluss* created the strategic conditions for Hitler to move against neighbouring Czechoslovakia, and in May he used the pretext of its government's mistreatment of the German-speaking minority in the Sudetenland to threaten invasion. The ensuing crisis generated intense popular anxiety in Germany and across Europe. It was not resolved until the Munich Agreement of 30 September, when a bellicose and enraged Hitler was forced to accept a compromise brokered and guaranteed by Britain, France, and Italy. Despite the cession of the Sudetenland, Hitler saw Munich as a mortifying setback to be reversed as soon as possible. Since most Germans were simply relieved that war had been averted, the press was instructed to rally them behind the harsh idea that peace was not eternal, that Germany was now threatened by a malignant coalition of enemies orchestrated by international Jewry.

Map 2. Germany. Territorial acquisitions and frontier changes to March 1939.

The Munich Agreement was duly tossed aside in March 1939, when Hitler leveraged Slovak separatism into a weapon for dismembering what was left of Czechoslovakia (Map 2). This was now war in all but name. Hitler's flagrant duplicity prompted Britain and France to issue a guarantee to Poland, where Germany was trying to extort fresh concessions on the minority question. Months of diplomatic activity followed, in an atmosphere suffused with miscalculation and distrust. If all major parties—France, Britain, Poland, the Soviet Union—were urgently seeking security wherever it might be found, there was a singular difference in Germany's case. Hitler's strategy lay not in stabilizing an incipient crisis, but in using it to create the optimum conditions for war. As he planned the assault on Poland, Hitler had to accept that simultaneous conflict in the west would now be virtually inevitable—but he was also able to win a stunning prize that would secure the eastern front after Poland's defeat and allow the Wehrmacht to turn safely westward. On 23 August, Nazi Germany and Soviet Russia concluded an astonishing non-aggression pact, accompanied by a secret agreement delineating respective 'spheres of interest' in Poland and the Baltic states. Buying time and benefits for both parties, the pact was the prelude to invasion.

Since 1936, European powers had been subjected to a crash course in the scope of German ambitions, the limits of their own political imagination, and the extent of their failures and mistakes. Germany's shattering invasion of Poland on 1 September 1939 brought victory within five weeks and the partition of the country with the Soviet Union. It was the epitome of a *Blitzkrieg* and was intended to be the latest in the series of Germany's contained confrontations. That we can now recognize it as the first step into global conflagration was due to the refusal of Poland, Britain, and France to consider peace on any other terms than the restoration of Poland's integrity and independence. It was due also to Britain's stubborn resistance even after the crushing blows of Germany's rapid successes in Denmark, Norway, Belgium, Holland, and France in the spring of 1940. Hitler's triumphs of

1939–40 were not 'cheap'—they cost the lives of almost 55,000 German soldiers—but they were the breath-taking pay-off of a huge military gamble which transferred virtually the whole of western Europe into Axis hands: a ready-made empire acquired in a matter of months. But they did not include Britain, whose defences and industrial capacity the Luftwaffe tried in vain to destroy between June 1940 and March 1941. The planned invasion never took place; the war in the west remained unfinished, shadowing Hitler's ambitions in the east.

Chapter 8
War

Conquest 1940–1942

With the invasion of Poland, Hitler had already embraced the risk that political and military logic would lead from contained campaigns to a general war. A year later, he had reached the point where the prize of unassailable German dominance in Europe and an open path in the east seemed within reach and outweighed all other risks. His directive issued to the Wehrmacht on 18 December 1940 to prepare 'Operation Barbarossa', the invasion of the Soviet Union, was premised on a delusory confidence that the Soviet army—which had lost 90 per cent of its top officers to Stalin's purges—would be annihilated at one stroke. Germany would conquer Russia's immense resources, now critical to its war economy. Britain would finally concede defeat, and the risk of US intervention would vanish. Germany would be the uncontested master of Europe up to the Russian steppes, and, as Hitler boasted in May 1943, 'To dominate Europe will be to assume the leadership of the world.'

The invasion was delayed by serious diversions in Greece, where Germany's ally Italy was facing defeat, and in the Balkans and North Africa: regions that remained the locus of intricate political, economic, and military entanglements for both Axis and Allies throughout the war. But on 22 June 1941, more than three million

German soldiers, stiffened by contingents from Germany's allies, poured across the frontiers. On the eve of invasion, Hitler told Mussolini that, having reached his decision, 'I do not entertain a second's doubt... I again felt spiritually free.' Yet the decision was also paradoxical evidence of the impasse into which Hitler had led Germany's dangerously stretched economic and military forces: only the conquest of new resources would enable Germany to continue its wars.

The Wehrmacht's drive deep into a shocked and unprepared Soviet Union seemed to justify Hitler's confidence, but within two months it was becoming clear that there was to be no repetition of the 1939/40 *Blitzkriege*. Instead, the invasion launched a prolonged and devastating war along a thousand-mile front, which brought staggering military losses on both sides: over half a million Wehrmacht casualties in the first three months alone, over four million in the Red Army by December.

Bedevilling the prosecution of the war was Hitler's refusal to heed the advice of his general staff, resulting in the resignation of the army commander-in-chief Walther von Brauchitsch in December 1941 and Hitler's personal assumption of this role. This was another risky flight of power to the apex of an already unbalanced regime. It took place just days after two other momentous events: Japan's attack on Pearl Harbor (7 December), its invasion of Europe's south-east Asian colonies, and Hitler's declaration of war on the USA (11 December). This pre-emptive move brought Germany strategic naval advantages and bound the Axis powers more tightly together, but it was also premised on Hitler's assumption that a disarmed and divided USA did not pose an immediate threat. But before this illusion was exposed, the Wehrmacht was able to mount a major new offensive in Russia in the spring of 1942, rolling the frontier of German power to the edge of the Caucasus oilfields and the gates of Stalingrad.

Occupation

Nazi dominion reached its greatest extent in 1942, with power to determine the lives and deaths of some 250 million people. Its remit ran from the pre-war annexations to the carcass of Poland and the Baltic states, the nations of western Europe acquired in 1940, and the parts of south-eastern Europe and of Russia that fell under German control in 1941–2. The term 'occupation' cannot capture the great variety of regimes imposed on these conquests or the fates of their inhabitants. They ranged from the annexation and integration of already partly Germanized regions—for example, Luxembourg or parts of western Poland—to the juridical limbo of the Polish 'General Government' region, or the hands-off regime in Denmark. In between were all manner of civil and military administrations, collaborationist regimes, and protectorates, the whole ringed by Germany's puppet states and allies in central Europe and the Balkans (Map 3).

Overriding the variety of local political frameworks was the stark differentiation between western and eastern Europe under Nazi rule. Western Europe was largely spared from active fighting after mid-1940, while the east, far from becoming the pacified colony anticipated by the Nazis, remained a virtually permanent war zone. Most of the 'Germanic' and 'kindred' peoples of western Europe experienced the relative stability of occupation far longer than the miseries of outright war, and this was amplified by the very different impact of Nazi racial principles. The east was a theatre of lawlessness, where—unlike in western Europe—violence, freelance plunder, and rape on the part of Wehrmacht and SS troops were normalized and generally went unpunished. Soviet civilian deaths would eventually far outstrip even the sickening total of their military casualties: this was not 'collateral damage' but the intended consequence of Nazi imperialist priorities. By contrast, the massacre of thousands of black prisoners of war from the French army in 1940 was a telling exception. Although all of Europe was treated as a source of slave labour (masterminded by Sauckel in his role as plenipotentiary for labour deployment) and subjected to the Nazis' genocidal antisemitism, the east was the preserve of an all-out racial war that engulfed not only its Jewish inhabitants but also 'inferior' Polish, Slav, and 'Gypsy' populations. Even under a regime of selective repression, persecution, and deportation, the majority of non-Jewish western Europeans were exempted from this scale of barbarity.

The same regional difference was felt in the crucial arena of economic exploitation. All occupied countries were subordinated to the demands of the German war economy and home front, but not in the same way. The advanced industrial societies of western Europe had a legitimacy and future of sorts under German tutelage: hence the plans for an integrated European economic zone and a political and cultural New Order, intended to unite Europe into a German-led confederation standing against both Soviet communism and American capitalism. Pending this reorganization of the geopolitical map, western European countries were most valuable to Germany if their economies and workforces could be taken under German control and exploited rationally and efficiently. The ambitious young experts who staffed German ministries, the SS, and the private sector designed highly sophisticated mechanisms of supervision, expropriation, taxation, and currency manipulation to procure raw materials, manufactures, agricultural produce, and profits on radically one-sided terms. Local production facilities as well as plunder were used not only to cover the costs of occupation, but to supply Germany's war machine with infrastructure and arms and its population with food. From France alone, products worth 154 billion francs poured into German hands by 1944, everything from artillery, cars, locomotives, and rolling stock to textiles, electrical equipment, and furniture. To the delight of their families, soldiers could send home packages of food and clothing procured at artificially low exchange rates, or simply stolen. This was

Map 3. The Nazi empire in Autumn 1942.

rationalized pillage on an industrial scale, with ample scope for profit-seeking, individual corruption, and self-enrichment.

Multiplied across Europe, this booty was essential to sustain Germany's war effort, but it distorted the economies and hammered the living standards of those who produced it. The economic imperative and its concomitant of increasingly harsh rule soon overrode any real possibility of either *Grossraumwirtschaft* or New Order. The public memory of these occupations is dominated by the bleak experience of ignominious defeat and German dominion, the seesaw of collaboration and resistance, the drumbeat of Gestapo terror, and the mass persecution and deportation of Jews and 'Gypsies'. Resistance in most western countries focused less on partisan warfare than on building and preserving underground networks to collect intelligence and mount targeted acts of sabotage pending liberation; only in the east was partisan resistance an adjunct to military warfare. Throughout Europe, individuals and small groups risked death to aid and protect the hunted and persecuted. Less willingly recalled is the extent to which Nazi rule was welcomed by political sympathizers and rested on the collaboration of local administrative and security personnel. Its more intimate counterpart was fraternization, a sexualized pejorative characteristically applied to women. Neither term can capture the full spectrum of choices made by those living through the long years of foreign domination: the self-serving pursuit of ambition, the temptation to trade integrity for security, the tiny infractions of German rules that preserved a sense of personal honour, the genuine intimacies that buckled the barrier between invader and vanquished.

Race war

By contrast with the west, less developed Poland, the Baltic region, and western Russia became the site of a catastrophic confluence of economic ruination, social devastation, and racial engineering. Here the role of Himmler and the SS far outstripped either the military or civilian administration, ensuring a colonial occupation based primarily on terror. Although German rule everywhere required the cooperation of local institutions and individuals, the Nazis had little interest in preserving the political integrity or fostering the backward agrarian economies of 'primitive' and 'inferior' Slav populations. Instead, German exploitation depended on systematic plunder and draconian repression. Raw materials and workers were hauled away to Germany, while local food supplies were reserved for the Wehrmacht or dispatched to Germany and western Europe. The chillingly detailed 'Hunger Plan' drawn up by German agricultural experts in the spring of 1941 calmly anticipated that tens of millions of Russian civilians and prisoners of war would have to starve to death if Germany's own wartime needs were to be met.

These visions of ruthless economic exploitation combined with the intensifying race war to turn the east into Europe's slaughterhouse. For these were not simply occupied countries: they were supposed to be the nucleus of a new German empire outlined in the so-called Master Plan for the East (*Generalplan Ost*) developed in the RSHA between 1940 and 1942. This programme for wholesale ethnic cleansing and colonization envisaged an extension of militarily secured German *Lebensraum* to the edge of the Urals. International law was violated by the dismemberment of states and the ruthless war against their allegedly dangerous but racially 'inferior' peoples: the destruction of their elites, the degradation of their non-Jewish populations, and the extermination of their Jewish inhabitants (see Chapter 9). Bearing the brunt of all this, the Poles were nullified as a state and a people, with Himmler masterminding this vision as Hitler's 'Commissioner for the Strengthening of the German Nation'. Western districts—where 85 per cent of the population was Polish and even Polish Jews outnumbered Germans—were annexed to the Reich, to be hastily Germanized by the resettlement of ethnic Germans. A Jewish reservation was planned for the east; and between them lay a residual dependency, the General Government ruled by Hans

Frank, into which the entire Polish population of the annexed districts would in theory be deported. In 1939, the Wehrmacht repressed residual Polish resistance with ruthless violence, while SD task forces (Einsatzgruppen) established by Heydrich liquidated the Polish leadership elites and intelligentsia, and let loose the first mass executions of Jews. But the mammoth task of ethnic transfer and resettlement defeated Himmler's bureaucrats; instead, racially eligible Poles were selected *in situ* for forcible Germanization, and the rest reduced to a helot class.

The Nazis construed the subsequent war against the USSR even more starkly as a war of ethno-political extermination: in Hitler's words, in March 1941, not just an armed struggle but 'a conflict between two ideologies [in which] the Jewish-Bolshevik intelligentsia...must be eradicated'. The so-called 'criminal orders' issued by Hitler and his generals in May and June 1941 gave free rein for Wehrmacht troops to eliminate alleged Soviet commissars, partisans, saboteurs, 'Asiatic' Red Army soldiers and prisoners of war, and Jews. Wehrmacht soldiers readily assimilated this authorization and the ideology behind it, or at least the sense that they were facing a pitiless enemy; they conducted the war in Russia with a barbarity unparalleled in western Europe. The role of Himmler and the SS in the occupied areas moved rapidly from imposing security by terror to committing mass murder and planning population transfers on an unprecedented scale, in preparation for the German racial New Order. But, as we shall see in Chapter 9, the only element of the Nazis' race war to come anywhere near success was not the grandiose dream of colonial subjugation and ethnic transformation, but the squalid nightmare of genocide.

War comes home 1943–1944

The Wehrmacht's disastrous reverse in Stalingrad in the winter of 1942/3, with the loss of 250,000 soldiers, was followed by the epic tank battle of Kursk that was the real turning point of the war.

Germany was now not just on the defensive but on the cusp of retreat, and not only in Russia but also in the face of Allied successes in North Africa, the Atlantic, and the Mediterranean. These included the Allied landings in Sicily and Italy in July–August 1943—the first breach of 'Fortress Europe'—which led to the downfall of Hitler's ally Mussolini. Subsequent tactical recoveries could not disguise the fact that Germany's forces were overextended, its resources dwarfed by the Allies', and its leadership bereft of any viable military or political strategy either to prosecute or end the conflict. Despite Hitler's wariness of provoking unrest by imposing excessive burdens on the German civilian population, Goebbels now led demands within the regime that the Führer had no choice but to embrace a strategy of total war. In an extraordinary propaganda performance staged in Berlin on 18 February 1943, Goebbels enlisted the wild acclamation of his audience as he enumerated every sacrifice that was needed to win this existential crusade against Jewish-Bolshevik chaos.

By then the war had already crept ineluctably home. The Allies' bombing campaign had escalated in 1942 into regular attacks on German cities, including a terrifying thousand-bomber raid on Cologne on 31 May which left 5,500 dead and injured and around 100,000 homeless. In 1943, round-the-clock raids by massed fleets of Allied aircraft—described in German propaganda as 'terror raids' by 'pirates and gangsters'—became the norm. Previous standards of destruction were dwarfed by the catastrophic fire-bombing of Hamburg in July, in which 35,000 people perished. Bombs were targeted not only at industrial and transport facilities but also at residential districts, aiming to cause mass homelessness and disrupt the labour supply—mocking Göring's boast that his Luftwaffe would preserve the homeland inviolate. The regime diverted fighter planes and anti-aircraft equipment and personnel to the defence of German air space, at the heavy price of further depleting the chronically undersupplied Russian front.

The war hit home in other ways too, the most obvious being the disruption of family life. Men of all ages disappeared into military and civil conscription; young women were dispatched to work on the land, to welfare work with newly 'Germanized' families in the annexed territories, or to serve in flak batteries. Hundreds of thousands of children were evacuated from cities within reach of Allied bombers to the safer countryside, including Thuringia—now not just Germany's 'Green Heart' but nominated by Sauckel as its 'Resistance Gau' (*Trutzgau*). The SD assiduously monitored the volatile movements of popular opinion, reporting on people's reactions to everything from the military situation and Hitler's increasingly rare public speeches, to changes in ration allocations or the treatment of Jews. Information about what was unfolding in the east—the mass murder of Jews as well as the Wehrmacht's parlous situation—could not be stifled, even though 'defeatism', listening to foreign radio stations, and rumour-mongering were treated with increasing severity. Death sentences, already averaging eighty-seven a year between 1933 and 1938, shot up to 5,336 in 1943. Acts of courageous open resistance, such as the sabotage or leafleting organized by underground communist cells or the White Rose group at the University of Munich, were rare; but members of the conservative-nationalist elites and pre-Nazi political activists, appalled at the progress of the war, coalesced into several clandestine circles to plan a national government for a negotiated post-Nazi future.

While the Nazi regime portrayed the homeland as a safe space protected by its front-line warriors, a growing proportion of its population was no longer even German. With eighteen million men drafted into the Wehrmacht and limits to the mobilization of German women, almost eight million foreigners were working alongside Germans in agriculture and industry by 1944. Concentration-camp inmates, including Jews, were drafted to the dangerous and publicly visible task of clearing bodies, rubble, and unexploded bombs after air raids. The regime that had devoted itself to racially purifying German society found itself importing millions of 'aliens' and 'inferiors' into the heart of the *Volksgemeinschaft*—exactly the alleged security threat that had alarmed Himmler and Heydrich. Concomitantly, by 1944 the Nazis' racial ambitions in eastern Europe collapsed into free fall as millions of desperate ethnic German refugees poured across the borders ahead of the advancing Soviet armies.

The end, 1944–1945

In 1944, as the progress of the Allied campaigns intent on forcing Germany's unconditional surrender met the desperate resistance of armies commanded by an intransigent Nazi leadership, Germans faced the full enormity of their looming fate. June brought not only the long-expected Allied invasion of France but the fall of Rome and immensely destructive Soviet offensives along fronts from Finland to Romania. Before the end of the year, Germany's borders had been breached east and west. But the regime's insistence on resistance to the bitter end brought unprecedented and senseless casualties precisely at the moment when there was no longer any prospect of a German victory. Over two and a half million German soldiers—half the total German military losses in the entire war—lost their lives in the ten months between July 1944 and May 1945, and most of the 400,000 civilian victims of Allied air raids were killed in the same period.

Despite Hitler's increasingly spectral leadership, the Nazi regime was not only intransigent but immovable. In a parodic inversion of the stab-in-the-back myth of 1918, the regime was shaken in July 1944 not by Hitler's nightmare of civilian unrest but by an army officers' plot to assassinate him. The attempt failed, but it vindicated Hitler's inveterate loathing of the military and conservative elites, and drove him into an even more narcissistic and apocalyptic unreality. The circle of plotters was sadistically liquidated, and the humiliated military leadership reduced to craven paralysis. Political authority was channelled into a gang of four—Goebbels, Himmler, Bormann, and Speer—charged with the remorseless mobilization of human and material resources. Hitler's apparently miraculous survival enhanced his preternatural aura in the eyes of a people desperate for salvation. The same craving nourished hopes that the V-1 and V-2 rockets, the *Vergeltungswaffen* (revenge weapons) launched from June 1944, would also force an end to the war.

The Nazi leadership secured people's continuing participation in this increasingly hopeless military struggle less by inculcating ideological enthusiasm than by declaring that there was no other choice and crushing all signs of defeatism. This message hit home hardest among those defending Germany from the Soviet Red Army, whose atrocities now made front-page news. The lesson Germans took from the barrage of propaganda was mixed: that the war was essentially defensive, forced onto Germany by 'Judeo-Bolshevik' aggressors, but also that they were now being punished for the regime's atrocities against the Jews. Commandeering people's embattled sense of personal survival and patriotic honour, the regime aimed to convert the fraying *Volksgemeinschaft* into something more symptomatic of the hour: a *Schicksalsgemeinschaft*, a community bound by fate, enlisting unquestioned sacrifice from all.

As the distinction between front line and homeland became increasingly illusory in 1945, the mass of Germans suffered and endured, while a core of Nazi believers fell back onto a savagely intensified invocation of the myth of their party's 1923 putsch, of blood sacrifice and the power of pure will to master history. Untrained boys and old men were forced to fight in the Volkssturm, the 'people's storm' brigades; local communities were exposed to the terror wrought by SS men and party officials intent on eliminating 'defeatists'. Thousands of Germans more rational than their desperate overlords were killed in this final slaughter; many more were murdered in prisons and concentration camps or perished in death marches as inmates were evacuated to the interior of Germany. In Weimar, the Gestapo executed their remaining prisoners in April 1945 and shot 'defeatists', deserters, and looters en masse. Like many other Nazi officials, Gauleiter Sauckel and his entourage contrived to flee; his city was fortunate in negotiating its surrender on 12 April, sparing it from the destruction inflicted on other communities where fanatics insisted on fighting to the end.

The Nazi regime came to an end twice: once with the Führer's suicide on 30 April, and again a week later with Germany's official capitulation on 8 May. The first act made the second possible, although not inevitable, as Hitler's designated successors attempted last-ditch negotiations for something less than unconditional surrender. But just as the Führer's suicide brought his regime to a squalid denouement, so the war culminated in Germany's total humiliation, exposing the full magnitude of its crimes to a horrified world.

Chapter 9
From terror to genocide

War sheltered the worst of the Nazis' crimes. The ideological and political scaffolding that supported them had been under construction since 1933; it had fostered a relativization of human value that corrupted the architects and agents of Nazi policy, and lent their lethal enterprises a spurious rationale derived from Nazi racial and biological 'science'. But that these structures would ultimately underpin genocide had not been inevitable. It was war that provided the impetus and the opportunity for the attempted physical extermination of Europe's Jewish populations, and it carried forward and linked the fates of the other targets of Nazi persecution and terror: concentration camp inmates, 'surplus' and 'inferior' populations of all kinds. War sanctioned and normalized mass terror and mass murder, blunted ethical reservations, and emphasized the insignificance of individual lives compared with the survival of the 'Aryan' race and utopian visions of its future.

Concentration camps

The bedrock of Nazi terror was the concentration camp network, as we saw in Chapter 4. By 1939, the camps were already foreshadowing the paradigm of terror, exploitation, and mass death that came to characterize the wartime system. The first foreign political prisoners from Austria and the Sudetenland arrived in the camps in 1938, the advance guard of the internationalized camp population that accelerated as Nazi conquests expanded. The overcrowding and ferocious mistreatment suffered by the 26,000 Jewish inmates detained in the November 1938 pogrom anticipated the camps' uncontrolled wartime expansion and brutalization. Finally, ongoing mass round-ups of the 'work-shy' were not only intended to intimidate German workers, but also pointed to the sinister new economic role given to the camps in the expanding SS empire.

The war brought a deadly synergism between terror, slave labour, and mass death in an SS empire that became more lethal as it proliferated. The camps' wartime expansion was driven as much by the SS's interest in the ballooning demand for labour as by strict security concerns. Their transformation into sources of SS economic power and reservoirs of forced labour for the war economy was sealed in February 1942, when Oswald Pohl's reorganized SS Head Office for Business and Administration (WVHA) took over control of the concentration camps. The economic model soon shifted from SS-owned factories located within the main camps to a more flexible deployment of slave labour in countless satellite compounds located next to industrial plants or construction sites. By 1943, as the regime committed Germany to total war, some two-thirds of camp inmates were working in the war economy, rented out to big industrial companies like IG Farben, Heinkel, and Siemens, to dozens of smaller employers, and to SS and state-owned enterprises. Three thousand of Buchenwald's inmates slaved nearby in the 'Fritz Sauckel' and 'Wilhelm-Gustloff' armaments factories (Figure 7).

Driven by the insatiable demand for labour and with European nations falling wholesale under Nazi control, the composition, size, and conditions of the camps' population were transformed during the war. They became the destination for prisoners of war, resisters, undesirables, offenders, and recalcitrants of every kind from occupied Europe, while Germans became a diminishing minority—in Buchenwald, their proportion fell from one-third in

Kraftomnibuslinie Weimar - Buchenwald

Fahrplan gültig ab 20. Mai 1942

1	3	5	7	9	11	13	15	17			2	4	6	8	10	12	14	16	18
Mi Sa So		Mi Sa So	So So				So So		ab		Mi So So	Mi So So	So So					So So	
9⁰⁰	12²⁰	13³⁰	15⁰⁰	16⁴⁰	18¹⁰	22²⁰	23²⁰	0³⁰	Weimar Sophienstiftsplatz an		10⁴⁰	13³⁰	14³⁰	16¹⁰	17⁴⁵	19¹⁵	23³⁰	0²⁰	1²⁰
9³⁵	12²⁵	13³⁵	15⁰⁵	16⁴⁵	18¹⁵	22²⁵	23²⁵	0³⁵	Weimar Cubenbecherstraße		10³⁵	13³⁵	14³⁰	16⁰⁵	17¹⁰	19¹⁰	23¹⁵	0¹⁵	1¹⁵
9⁴⁵	12³⁵	13⁴⁵	15¹⁵	16⁵⁵	18²⁵	22³⁵	23³⁵	0⁴⁵	Prinzenschneise		10²⁵	13¹⁵	14²⁰	15⁵⁵	17²⁰	19⁰⁰	23⁰⁵	0⁰⁵	1⁰⁵
10⁰⁰	12⁵⁰	14⁰⁰	15³⁰	17¹⁰	18⁴⁰	22⁵⁰	23⁵⁰	0⁴⁰	Lager Buchenwald an ab		10¹⁰	13⁰⁰	14⁰⁵	15⁴⁰	17¹⁵	18⁴⁵	22⁵⁰	23⁵⁰	0⁵⁰

Zeichenerklärung:
Mi — Mittwochs, Sa — Sonnabends, So — Sonn- und Feiertags, W — Werktags
(— verkehrt nicht täglich, Mo—Fr — Montags bis Freitags

Omnibus-Verkehrs-Gesellschaft m. b. H. Weimar

Ruf 3500   Theaterplatz 1b   Ruf 3500

7. Timetable for the regular bus service between Weimar and Buchenwald in May 1942; the final stop is 'Buchenwald Camp'. The city's residents were also familiar with prisoner convoys and columns of inmates working in the city.

1942 to less than 10 per cent in 1944. Women, a small minority in 1939, amounted to 28 per cent of inmates by January 1945 as their labour too was sucked into the war economy. The total population of the main camps and their satellites doubled every year between 1939 and 1944; from 21,400 in September 1939 it had reached over 524,000 by mid-1944, and increased to at least 714,000 at the start of 1945.

Concentration camps were not extermination camps, but they were steeped in death. Conditions of life before 1939 had been punitive and degrading, yet not generally lethal; but as the war proceeded, the expanded network could not cope with the accelerating influx of detainees or the chaotic traffic of labour allocation and transfer. The radical deterioration in basic facilities—accommodation, food, medical care—along with brutal discipline, inhumane punishments, and relentless labour exacted a corresponding toll in misery and lives. Systemically deficient planning and management were symptomatic of the SS culture of contempt for inmates they regarded as barely human. Tens of thousands were deliberately put to death when they became unable to work, or perished as a result of medical experiments. In the final months of the war, the bloated concentration camp system in effect imploded in a final catastrophe of disorder and mass death. 'I don't want to die like this', wrote the Yugoslav Jewish communist Hanna Lévy-Hass, starving in the unimaginable conditions of Bergen-Belsen in April 1945. 'It would be better to die right away, as quickly as possible…like a human being…we don't die here, we rot to death…What a disgrace, what an immense disgrace.' By 1945, over 1.7 million men, women, and children had perished in these camps, the great majority after 1942.

From persecution to planned murder

Death was a wanton by-product of the SS concentration camps, but it was the explicit objective of other programmes devoted to the mass murder of populations the Nazis defined as superfluous, inferior, or dangerous. Once the threshold to mass murder was breached in 1939, a grotesque dynamic of escalation and diversification ensued, responding to newly emerging horizons and opportunities, feeding grand visions and individual ambitions alike. Different actors and agencies within the Nazi universe, sharing a bundle of utilitarian, eugenic, and racial principles, initiated programmes of killing with overlapping goals and methods, and established institutional mechanisms for their implementation. The most seductive camouflage for these initiatives was the facile Nazi precept that the welfare of the *Volksgemeinschaft* overrode the needs and rights of individual Germans, as well as all those outside the implacable boundaries of the *Volk*.

'Euthanasia'

The first victims of systematic mass murder were mentally and physically handicapped Germans. This group had long been regarded by some leading Nazis and medical authorities as a physical danger and a drain on national resources; the rationale of war provided the final legitimation for action. 'Euthanasia' was an utterly corrupt euphemism for the mass actions carried out in 1939–41 to purge Germany's biological and racial stock, to cull people incapable of contributing to the economy, and to free medical facilities for military use. It began in July 1939, when Hitler authorized the killing of a severely handicapped newborn whose parents had appealed to him to grant their child a 'mercy death' (*Gnadentod*). This released a series of murderous initiatives against mentally and physically handicapped infants and adults. A further confidential instruction signed by Hitler in October 1939 empowered designated physicians to 'vouchsafe a mercy death' to adults judged 'incurably ill'. It soon escalated into a nationwide operation by medical bureaucrats and physicians to identify and register all psychiatric patients judged incapable of work, as well as asylum inmates who were deemed criminally insane or 'non-German'—meaning Jewish or 'Gypsy'.

As the war began, a secret operation, codenamed T-4, took up the task of selecting and killing the victims; by the end of the war they numbered at least 100,000, including 5,000 children. The process of selection, authorization, and delivery to killing sites was bureaucratically meticulous. Alongside poison and starvation, suffocation by carbon monoxide gas was found to be the most efficient method of large-scale killing. Gas chambers—the first of their kind—were constructed in designated killing centres to which patients were delivered as if for medical care. These operations were shrouded in secrecy, and official communications referred to the killing evasively as 'mercy death' and 'treatment' (*Behandlung*); but given the number of families, bureaucrats, and medical staff involved, full confidentiality was impossible. The programme aroused deep public disquiet and unprecedented levels of open protest, mainly on religious grounds. Hitler had long been wary of this possibility, and in August 1941, with the initial killing quotas reached, he ordered the programme to be scaled back.

But this was not the end of T-4 or murder by gas. Selective 'euthanasia' killings continued in Germany, while Himmler had already arranged for the SS to use T-4 gas chambers to resolve a crisis of overcrowding and sickness in the concentration camps by killing inmates too weak to work. By the time this programme was scaled back in the spring of 1942, the culling of enfeebled inmates had been normalized and the principle of 'selection' for work or death was written into the practice of the concentration and labour camps. Similar techniques had also been adopted by a special SS unit, commanded by Herbert Lange, dedicated to killing asylum and hospital patients in occupied Poland from 1939. Personnel and expertise from these operations were soon to be diverted to even more horrifying and extensive campaigns of extermination.

The 'final solution'

Let us start with language. Eight months before the invasion of Poland, in the course of a lengthy speech on 30 January 1939 marking the sixth anniversary of his appointment as chancellor, Hitler uttered a now infamous 'prophecy' to which he and others in his entourage would refer repeatedly in the coming years:

> If international finance Jewry inside and outside Europe succeeds in plunging the nations into another world war, then the result will be not the bolshevization of the globe and with it the victory of Jewry, but the annihilation [*Vernichtung*] of the Jewish race in Europe.

The sentiment is clear, but its evasive language is instructive. Unlike a direct threat, Hitler's 'prophecy' of annihilation displaces agency and process to an unspecified realm of self-activating events. It sidesteps responsibility, anticipates without enunciating, and conjures erasure without committing to its meaning or realization. The Nazis' 'Jewish question', presented here as an existential threat, would only be resolved with the disappearance of 'the Jews'; but, when opportunity presented itself in 1939, what did this mean?

The terms commonly used today—the Holocaust, Shoah, genocide—give a deceptive retrospective unity to something that at the time had not acquired this integral shape, let alone this language. Even the eventual definition of the preferential Nazi term *Endlösung*, the 'final solution' of the 'Jewish question', was shrouded in equivocation. The word came into circulation among SS planners towards the end of 1939, distinguishing immediate actions against Jews in Poland from hazy longer-term plans for 'evacuating' Jews into a distant reservation after the war. Its full phantasmic potential broke the surface only in 1941/2, when it became the sickening euphemism that is now indissoluble from the Nazis' most infamous crime against humanity: the attempted extermination of the Jewish people. But evasion and euphemism did not monopolize Nazi language. Alongside them and in public circulated grossly physical characterizations of 'the Jew' as vermin, bacillus, disease—poisonous life forms fit only for eradication. Missing in both styles is any conception of the millions of human beings who would have to be individually 'annihilated'.

Previous chapters have discussed the place of antisemitism in Nazi ideology and the violent persecution of Jewish Germans after 1933. The primary task here is to examine how, after 1939, the Nazis found the ability to countenance annihilating an entire people and the means to accomplish it. War and conquest repeatedly augmented the number of Jews living in German-controlled territories, and brought serial 'Jewish questions' for 'solution' in the different territories of Germany, Poland, western Europe, and the Soviet Union. Gathering the threads into an overarching policy of wholesale extermination, carried out in the death camps of occupied Poland and the killing fields of the Soviet Union, was a spasmodic and improvised process.

Hitler's racial obsessions framed what could be envisaged and enacted by others, but historians agree that it is pointless to look for a recorded extermination order from Hitler, comparable to the euthanasia order, or for a blueprint for its execution. Hitler's objectives were instead communicated through an often oblique verbal repertoire of expectation, endorsement, and authorization. For those involved in realizing mass murder—Himmler, Heydrich, and other leading members of the regime; bureaucrats and Nazi personnel in Germany and the east; military, police, and SS commanders in the field—legitimacy depended as much on a common ideological consensus as on formal orders. Authority was sealed by the stabilization and sharing of assumptions that shifted the boundaries of the permissible to encompass the previously unsayable. By what might almost be termed a law of intended consequences, these mechanisms enabled the transition from policies of ghettoization, deportation, lethal neglect, and massacre to the final attempts at wholesale physical extermination. To understand this process, we therefore need to look not for clear programmatic instructions, but at a more uneven convergence of central decisions and local initiatives, at the wilful narrowing of alternatives, and the crumbling of inhibitions.

Deportation and 'ghettoization', 1939–1940

Directed by Heydrich, the RSHA's pre-war policy of forced emigration had partially exported the 'Jewish question' to countries beyond German jurisdiction. By December 1940, according to his subordinate Eichmann's calculations, half a million Jews (by Nuremberg Law definitions) had left the Greater German Reich (Germany, Austria, and the Protectorate of Bohemia and Moravia), but this left some 300,000 still resident. Although emigration continued to be encouraged until October 1941, most of these people were now trapped in the Reich. Crushed in a tightening vice of persecution—not only paralysing restrictions on everyday life but forced labour and segregation in ghetto-like 'Jewish houses' and makeshift camps—they lived a humiliating and destitute half-life on the fringes of largely hostile or indifferent populations, awaiting a desperately uncertain fate.

That fate had become more uncertain with the German occupation of Poland and the beginning of plans for mass deportations or 'resettlement' of Jews now in German hands. Who precisely was to be 'resettled', where, and with what final objective was not fixed from the start. The successive plans proposed or implemented by Himmler, Heydrich, and the RSHA between 1939 and 1942 responded to changing military and political considerations, to Hitler's decisions, and to the stalling or failure of previous schemes. Yet from the start, 'resettlement' plans carried the calculated expectation that victims would succumb to the cruel conditions of transfer and the brutalities of life and labour in desolate destinations.

The schemes drawn up by Heydrich immediately after the invasion of Poland envisaged that the 1.7 million Polish Jews who had fallen under German control would first be concentrated in local ghettos, pending plans to gather them at the eastern edge of German-occupied Poland. There, along with Jews from the Reich, 'Gypsies', and sundry undesirables, they would in theory await deportation further east as new territories fell to German conquest. This vast and inhuman plan was one strand in Himmler's strategic but frustrated project of racial engineering and territorial revision in Germany's new colonial heartland (see Chapter 8). Only fractions of the scheduled removals were achieved, at the expense of terrible suffering and mortality as deportees were trafficked eastwards to 'reservations' that were little more than waterlogged fields. By the spring of 1940, when these overwhelming logistical problems had caused the plan to be suspended, another opportunity briefly gained currency after the fall of France. Reviving an older antisemitic fantasy, the 'Madagascar Plan' proposed to banish Europe's Jews to this remote and controllable French colonial territory. The military situation rendered it unfeasible, but it reinforced the principle that all of Europe, west and east, would somehow be cleared of Jews by mass deportations.

As a result of these failures, ghettoization—what the RSHA called the establishment of closed 'Jewish residential areas'—proceeded unevenly in occupied Poland. It involved numerous violently enforced local population transfers as Jewish and Polish residents were removed from each other's designated spaces. Whether living inside or outside the jammed ghettos, Polish Jews were subject to systematic persecution. The Nazi authorities also made ghetto inmates complicit in their own fate by appointing community leaders responsible for internal administration and policing. With their regimes of arbitrary abuse, forced labour, and minimal rations, the ghettos might be seen as miniature anticipations of the post-war Jewish reservation.

One of the largest ghettos was established in April 1940 in Łodz, a centre of the textile industry in the annexed Wartheland with a pre-war Jewish population of 200,000. Renamed Litzmannstadt, this city was intended by its Nazi administrators to be rebuilt as a model of Germanic urban culture, and the ghetto's designation was justified in a specious language of town planning and public hygiene. A travesty of coexistence emerged. The ghetto became a grotesque 'model' in the eyes of its Nazi-appointed Jewish leader, Chaim Rumkowski, who exploited the view of some influential Nazi officials and businessmen that the German war economy needed to make rational use of the forced labour of Jews. Rumkowski aimed to make his ghetto indispensable, with the survival of its starving inhabitants contingent on their ability to work. What this meant when the first deportations began to destroy the life of the ghetto after January 1942 was recorded by a young inmate, Dawid Sierakowiak: 'The Germans are demanding all the children up to age ten, the elderly over sixty-five, and all other sick, swollen invalids, people unable to work, and those without employment. The panic in the city is incredible

... everyone's running to secure work assignments for those in their family who are unemployed.' The destination of the deportees was to be Chełmno, the first Nazi extermination camp.

War of extermination, 1941

As the situation of Polish Jews remained unresolved, the war Hitler launched against the Soviet Union in June 1941 ushered in a new and catastrophic phase of his war against the Jews. Hitler's propaganda condensation of 'the enemy' into the figure of 'Jewish Bolshevism' was now given a literal and ruthless interpretation. From the very start of the military campaign, enlarged SD Einsatzgruppen and police units, supported by Wehrmacht troops, unleashed a racial war against Jews who fell into German hands, most of them in the Ukraine and Belarus.

The precipitate descent into a spiral of utterly barbarous slaughter was authorized by Himmler, acting on Hitler's intentions; it was backed by the Wehrmacht's newly radicalized rules of engagement and accelerated by individual Einsatzgruppen commanders. The majority of these officers were not out-of-control sadists, but often educated and ambitious young professionals who had chosen to make rapid careers in the SS and SD. SS-Brigadeführer Otto Rasch, for example, held doctorates in law and economics; he commanded Einsatzgruppe C in the Ukraine, where he supervised the massacre of over 30,000 Jews at Babi Yar in September 1941. Mass reprisals and executions in the name of 'security' included increasing numbers of Jews, and SS and police units were soon authorized by Himmler to move on to wholesale massacres of Jewish men, women, and children. Most were then shot by the hundreds and thousands, often with the participation of local collaborationists. By August, entire Jewish communities in the conquered territories of western Russia were being murdered and districts declared 'free of Jews'. By the time the first cycle of killing came to an end in early 1942, it had already claimed 750,000 lives.

This scale of orchestrated mass murder was a new departure. It expanded what was morally thinkable and practically feasible in the universe of Nazi anti-Jewish policy. Nazi leaders had expected speedy victory in Russia to deliver limitless territory for both a new German 'Garden of Eden' cleansed of Jews, and a Jewish reservation in Siberia. At the end of July 1941, Göring, acting on Hitler's authority, accordingly charged Heydrich with preparing a *Gesamtlösung* (comprehensive solution) of 'the Jewish question' throughout the German sphere of influence in Europe. This was to take the form of 'emigration or evacuation when conditions permitted'—still meaning after the war—and the RSHA's expert Eichmann initiated immediate planning. But as victory began to elude the Wehrmacht and new problems piled up, anti-Jewish policy was caught between the slaughter raging in Russia and the self-imposed limbo in the Polish General Government and the Wartheland. There, to the mounting fury of governors Hans Frank and Arthur Greiser, millions of terrorized Jews and 'Gypsy' families were now marooned in desperate circumstances.

Their numbers were augmented in September 1941 when Hitler agreed to the resumption of deportations of Jews from the Reich, but not yet to their murder. Further emigration was banned and deportees were stripped of the vestiges of their citizenship so that their property could be legally seized by the German financial authorities as they were shipped across the frontier. Despite having wanted to postpone deportations from Germany and western Europe until the end of the war, Hitler had bowed to mounting pressure from Gauleiters who wanted their realms to become 'Jew-free' as soon as possible. Goebbels, Gauleiter of Berlin as well as propaganda minister, was the loudest of these voices for the immediate radicalization of anti-Jewish policy. In a vitriolic propaganda campaign in the second half of 1941, he aimed to stoke public rage against German Jews as a treacherous Bolshevik fifth column. It was at his insistence that Hitler, wary as ever of public reactions, finally agreed that German Jews should now be publicly stigmatized by yellow star badges.

The arrival in Poland and the 'Ostland' (the Nazi commissariat in the Baltic and Belarus regions) of Reich deportees whose further fate had not been decided added to the already building crisis. Unprepared authorities began radical improvisations to dispose of unfit or 'surplus' Polish Jews. In the Wartheland, where Łodz became the destination of 25,000 Reich Jews, Gauleiter Greiser arranged with Himmler that 100,000 local Polish Jews incapable of work would be subjected to 'special treatment'—now the euphemism for murder—as a quid pro quo for these unwelcome new arrivals. In Riga and Minsk, some deportees from the Reich were simply shot on arrival, without authorization. The local Gauleiter, Wilhelm Kube, who described himself as 'hard and ready to assist in the solution of the Jewish question', professed shock at the brutality of the slaughter and queried whether a more humane method could not be found for disposing of 'people from our own cultural milieu', as opposed to the 'native animalistic hordes' (a distinction shared by other Nazis). Himmler too was now investigating 'less cruel' methods than mass shooting; with the help of Lange's experts, a fixed site for mass murder by exhaust gas—the first death camp—was established in Chełmno, near Łodz, beginning its operations in December 1941.

An arc of death now spanned Poland. In Lublin, on the other side of the country, where Himmler had sent one of his most bloodstained SS chiefs, Odilo Globocnik, to launch a crash programme of racial engineering, Jews were being murdered en masse or worked to death in road-building camps. In November 1941, Himmler and Globocnik brought in T-4 specialists (equipped with gassing technologies 'improved' by experiments on concentration camp inmates) to advise on the construction of a death camp in Bełżec, near the Lublin ghetto. The 'temporary' ghettos of 1939/40 in occupied Poland were already overwhelmed by starvation and disease; Nazi authorities pondered, in the words of one RSHA official in July 1941, 'whether the most humanitarian solution would not be to finish off those Jews who are unfit for work by some expedient means'.

These terrifying initiatives were not yet part of a coordinated plan, but they marked a drastic escalation in the cumulative rationale, scale, and technology of death. Over the autumn and winter of 1941, this distinction began to be effaced. By the end of November, Heydrich was ready to report progress on Hitler's fiat for a pan-European 'final solution'. At the same time, the tone of Hitler's public and private declarations on the punitive fate in store for the Jews became yet more threatening, his indications of a drastic 'solution' more frequent. On 11 December 1941, Germany declared war on the United States. A day later, with Germany now locked in struggle against the forces of 'international Jewry' across two continents, Hitler took a gathering of top national and regional Nazi leaders into his confidence:

> As far as the Jewish question is concerned, the Führer is resolved to make a clean sweep. He had prophesied to the Jews that if they were to precipitate another world war, this would mean their annihilation. This was no empty phrase. The world war is here, the annihilation of the Jews will be the inevitable consequence. This question must be approached without any sentimentality.

Those present knew a boundary had been crossed. As Hans Frank briefed his senior officials in Kraków a few days later:

> But what's to happen to the Jews? Do you think they will be accommodated in village settlements?...Gentlemen, I must ask you to arm yourselves against any feelings of compassion. We must annihilate the Jews wherever we find them and wherever it is possible.

Genocide 1942–1945

Frank's report referred to 'major measures' about to be discussed in the Reich: these were the agenda of the Wannsee conference summoned by Heydrich, and named after the Berlin lakeside suburb where it was held on 20 January 1942. The participants included senior RSHA officials and SS officers already actively involved in mass murder; and state secretaries from the major Reich ministries, who were now forced to confront the dire consequences of their earlier achievements in the bureaucracy of persecution. The conference reviewed the pan-European scope of the Nazis' 'Jewish question' and the difficulty of including German part-Jews ('Mischlinge') and Jews in mixed marriages. Heydrich was concerned to ensure the cooperation and complicity of all government departments involved, while also asserting overall RSHA authority. He announced that emigration would be replaced by forced 'evacuation'. Able-bodied Jews were to be progressively deported to labour battalions in the east, where a large proportion was expected to 'fall away by natural depletion'. Those who did not—the elite of the 'hardiest'—would be 'dealt with appropriately' to prevent them becoming the 'nucleus of a Jewish resurgence'. So the connection between 'evacuation' and mass murder was drawn more tightly (Map 4).

The Wannsee conference provided the framework within which initiatives already in progress could be expanded and propelled into an explosive onward momentum. Between March 1942 and October 1943, 1.75 million mainly Polish Jews were gassed in the three so-called 'Reinhard Action' camps (the name commemorating Reinhard Heydrich after his assassination in June 1942). These death camps were established by Globocnik near to major ghettos: Bełżec and Sobibór near Lublin, and Treblinka near Warsaw; Chełmno continued to annihilate the Jewish population of Łodz and the Wartheland, and the camp of Majdanek near Lublin added to the killing power. Simultaneously, a renewed campaign of mass murder was launched in those regions of the occupied Soviet Union that had not already been 'cleared' of Jews in 1941. The vast majority were shot by the Einsatzgruppen or collaborationist squads. By the time the Red Army drove the Nazis from Soviet soil in 1944, an estimated two million Russian Jews had been slaughtered. Here neither bureaucracy nor technology were at work: just raw butchery.

Map 4. Eastern Europe under Nazi occupation.

The victims of the death camps included Jewish deportees from central Europe, and the first groups from western Europe. Some Jews from the Reich—the old and the sick, certain groups of 'Mischlinge'—were deported to the so-called 'old age ghetto' of Theresienstadt, but only as a stepping stone to the death camps. In May 1942, the last twenty-eight Weimar Jews were among 600 herded from across Thuringia into the cattle auction hall near the Weimar goods station, to be deported to their deaths in Bełżec and Majdanek. A few weeks later, a city official declared that 'Thank God, the Jewish breed has already become history here, now that the last children of Israel living in Weimar have been expelled with due force.'

It was another camp system, centred on Auschwitz in Upper Silesia, that became the destination for the majority of victims from western Europe. Auschwitz was a distinctive complex in the universe of Nazi camps, eventually combining overlapping functions on a uniquely large scale: it was a concentration camp for political prisoners and detainees, a labour camp for the giant IG Farben chemical works, and an extermination camp. The first contingent of Jewish victims, from Upper Silesia, was killed in the spring of 1942 with Zyklon-B, a cyanide gas first tested on Russian POWs the previous September. This was followed by a flow of train transports from across Europe, scheduled and staffed by regular rail personnel. By the time Auschwitz was abandoned in January 1945, a million Jews from across Europe had lost their lives there, alongside tens of thousands of non-Jewish Poles, Russians, and 'Gypsies'.

All the European states under Nazi occupation or in the Nazi sphere of influence subjected their Jewish populations to regimes of registration and persecution, whether imposed by the occupiers or adopted more or less voluntarily. These were the crucial mechanisms for identifying and capturing potential deportees, but the scope and the timing of their removal could not simply be dictated by Himmler or executed with bureaucratic expediency.

This depended on local political conditions and diplomatic considerations, and sometimes on the state of public opinion; survival rates too reflected these factors.

In the Netherlands, with its compact Jewish population, the grip of Nazi power converged with a national tradition of bureaucratic and civic discipline to produce a tragically efficient process of identification and deportation. Three-quarters of the pre-war Jewish population were murdered, the highest proportion in western Europe. Yugoslavia lost almost 80 per cent of its Jewish population as the fascist Ustasha regime, pursuing its own ethnic cleansing, murdered Serbian Jews en masse and delivered thousands of Croatian Jews to Auschwitz. In Denmark, by contrast, where German rule was largely indirect and the Jewish population numbered no more than 7,500, popular resistance enabled over 90 per cent to flee to the nearby territory of neutral Sweden. In France, with a pre-war Jewish population of 330,000, the Vichy government actively collaborated in the deportations. The most vulnerable were Jewish refugees who were not French citizens, while a majority of those who were survived. Germany's allies Romania, Hungary, and Bulgaria were reluctant to hand over their own citizens but also abandoned those without full political ties to the nation. In Hungary, it was only when the Nazis usurped power in March 1944 (as in Italy the previous year) that the deportations could begin, provoking a final paroxysm of killing in Auschwitz between May and July 1944 that extinguished over 300,000 lives.

Between deportation and death lay the faint chance of clinging to life as slave labour in the Reich and SS war economy. A small minority of Jews arriving in Auschwitz escaped the gas chambers, but their survival was then governed by the savage principle of 'selection' already pioneered in the German concentration camps. Those who did not perish from their appalling treatment were killed as soon as they became too weak to work: in some labour camps, life expectancy could be measured in weeks. Thus was fulfilled the cold-blooded Wannsee calculation that numerous Jewish lives would be lost in labour battalions by 'natural depletion'.

Resistance

The Nazis did not succeed in annihilating the Jewish people, but they did manage to destroy a centuries-old Jewish culture in its eastern European heartlands of Poland, Lithuania, Ukraine, and Belarus. The continental scale of the slaughter is scarcely conceivable: six million out of a pre-war European Jewish population of 9.4 million. As many were shot in the 'holocaust of bullets' in the shtetls and ghettos of eastern Europe and the Soviet Union as were shipped to the gas chambers that have become the emblem of the Holocaust.

The mind-numbing statistics of death risk submerging the many acts of individual and collective Jewish resistance, and of aid given by non-Jews. These acts were undertaken in the face of odds so overwhelming—not just the power of the Germans but the general indifference or hostility of surrounding populations—that most Jews were reluctant to defy their oppressors until all other hope was extinguished. The most famous collective action was the uprising in the Warsaw ghetto in April/May 1943, whose tenacity shocked the Germans. Resistance groups existed in many other ghettos and camps—even in Treblinka and Sobibór, where in the summer of 1943 the Jewish Sonderkommandos ('special squads' forced to assist with the killing process) organized revolts when it appeared that their camps were about to be liquidated. In October 1944, the Auschwitz-Birkenau Sonderkommando rose up in a similar act of desperate defiance. In Belarus, the renewed SS onslaught in 1943 met with armed Jewish resistance and organized flight, sometimes with the support of Soviet partisans and a non-Jewish population with little tradition of antisemitism.

Another form of resistance was less spectacular but of infinite importance at the time and since. This was the painful and risky task of writing down the histories and experiences of the calamity, smuggling them to safety, or hiding them for the chance of future discovery. They include the journals of individuals like Grigorij Schur in the Vilna ghetto, Dawid Sierakowiak in Łodz, or Hanna Lévy-Hass in Belsen; the desperate testimonies scrawled by a few members of the doomed Sonderkommandos; the archive collected by Emmanuel Ringelblum and the Oneg Shabbat group in Warsaw; and the monumental daily chronicle of the Łodz ghetto compiled by an officially appointed group of historians and archivists. These texts were written with the explicit aim of recording a history that the authors knew would otherwise be monopolized or expunged by the oppressors. 'It is difficult to hold a pen, to concentrate one's thoughts', wrote Chaim Kaplan in Warsaw in 1940. 'But… it is a duty I must perform. This idea is like a flame imprisoned in my bones, burning within me, screaming Record!'

Liberation

With the advance of Allied armies from east and west, the last phase of SS terror unfolded in January 1945. Hundreds of thousands of inmates of the camps in the east were evacuated westwards in horrifying 'death marches', intended to salvage workers for Germany, that descended into processions of lawless murder. By the time Soviet troops entered the remnants of the Auschwitz complex on 27 January 1945, they found no more than 7,000 sick and dying inmates. As in other sites across the landscape of genocide, the SS had made efforts to destroy the evidence—gas chambers, crematoria, mass graves, files.

Eleven weeks later, Buchenwald became the first major concentration camp in western Germany to be liberated. Its communist underground awaited the approach of US troops before giving the signal for the remaining 21,000 inmates to seize control (Figure 8). On 11 April 1945, as a US armoured column could be seen advancing towards the camp, the prisoners rose and

8. Barracks in Buchenwald after liberation in April 1945. Behind an effigy of Hitler on a gallows, inmates have painted the slogan 'Hitler must die so that Germany may live'.

chased the SS away. Five days later, the US military commander ordered a thousand Weimar citizens to be marched into Buchenwald 'in order to convince them of the conditions there before they are altered'. The challenge to Germans to confront the crimes committed in their name had been issued.

Epilogue: Coming to terms with the past

The arithmetic of wartime destruction in 1945 was mind-numbing. In lives, fifty-five million dead, the majority of them civilians, including twenty-seven million Soviet citizens, seven million Germans, and almost six million—60 per cent—of Europe's Jewish populations. In economic resources, two-thirds of transport systems and industrial plant destroyed in German-occupied Russia; 20 per cent of German housing rendered uninhabitable; agricultural production and coal output in Europe cut by half. In displaced populations, sixty million people severed from their homes, including eleven million German soldiers in Allied captivity and an eventual total of twelve million German refugees and expellees pouring in across the redrawn borders of eastern Europe. Families were in disarray, and in Germany the gender order was thrown into confusion as masculine authority was diminished by defeat and captivity and women were left to fend for themselves.

Contemporaries feared that the shock to civilization was irreparable and despaired of the task of moral as well as physical reconstruction. The economic and political response to that challenge—the history of reconstruction and the establishment of the two post-war German states—lies beyond the scope of this book. My epilogue returns to core questions raised in earlier chapters: the place of National Socialism in German history and what it meant to be 'German' after Nazism.

In Germany, relief at the end of wartime devastation and Nazi terror was accompanied by feelings of shame and rage at the deeds of the regime. Yet defeat, occupation, and partition brought challenges and disappointments that attenuated these responses. Germans' suffering in the shattering final months of the war vied with their willingness to acknowledge the torments they had inflicted on others. The immediate post-war years saw harsher living conditions than most Germans had known for much of the war, indeed since the later 1930s; by contrast, Hitler and his regime were credited with great achievements until the shocking turn of the war against Russia. 'Without Goebbels and Himmler and Bormann too, and others who only came later,' wrote Sauckel in his Nuremberg cell, facing execution for war crimes and crimes against humanity, 'Hitler would have been the luminary of German history.'

Germans could draw on their patterns of experience and memory as a yardstick to measure the privations of their lives after 1945; they lent suffering and victimhood a comparative dimension that defied the moral absolutes applied to National Socialism by the Allies. Victimhood was extended from those who had actually been persecuted by the Nazis to those who had suffered in other ways: in the Allied bombing war, on the Russian front, or as refugees and expellees from the east. The habit of turning a blind eye, cultivated by so many after 1933, now translated into repudiation of any guilt for the catastrophe. The Nazi period was widely represented as a historical anomaly, a 'road accident' or wrong turning that might have occurred anywhere, and that had dislodged the German nation from its expected historical path. Blaming the Allies for their alleged failings was part of this—not only for the miseries and inequities of the occupation regimes, but for pre-war foreign policies that had lent credibility to the appeal of National Socialism and helped stabilize Hitler's government.

Reporting on a visit to her native country in 1950, Hannah Arendt deplored what she saw as Germans' 'deep-rooted, stubborn, and at times vicious refusal to face and come to terms with what really happened'. My book is one bid to explain what had 'really happened' in Germany by 1945; but what would 'coming to terms' with this mean, historically and ethically? The victorious Allies made an initial effort between 1945 and 1949 to confront Germans with the historical reality of National Socialism through the trials of leading men in the Nazi government, the military, the Nazi Party, big business, and the professional elites. The International Military Tribunal (IMT) and subsequent proceedings under international law were intended to serve didactic as well as judicial purposes: not only to assign individuals' responsibility for planning and waging aggressive war and committing war crimes and crimes against humanity, but also to demonstrate precisely how these crimes had been enabled and committed.

By the end of 1949, the context for confronting or coming to terms with the Nazi past had been radically altered by the enveloping Cold War and the establishment of two separate states on German soil. With Austrian independence restored, the task of rebuilding German national identity and international standing fell separately to the East and West German governments within their respective alliances. Although both looked in theory to reunification, their societies were saturated by different readings of German history. Each Germany invoked its own version of this history in order to legitimate itself and inflict the burden of the Nazi past on the other. The West German Federal Republic (BRD) saw itself as the democratic inheritor of pre-Nazi German statehood and the antagonist of totalitarianism, Nazi or communist. The East German Democratic Republic (DDR) rested on the alternative authority of socialist anti-fascism and an older progressive lineage in German history, treating the BRD as Nazism's sole legatee.

In these circumstances, the public evaluation of National Socialism developed as an unusually intensive exchange between politics, academic history, and popular memory. The East German state's socialist project suggested, if not entirely accurately, a more complete rupture with the immediate past than in the BRD. It held many more trials than were mounted in the BRD, but its government strictly policed the scope of permitted scholarly and public debate, ensuring that the emphasis was placed on German anti-fascist resistance and on liberation by the Red Army. In West Germany, led until 1966 by conservative Christian Democrats (CDU) and their partners, the restoration of capitalism, the family, and liberal democracy relied on historical continuities which shielded the guilty from exposure and amounted, in the eyes of its critics, to a reprehensible accommodation with the legacy of National Socialism. Although this was accompanied by a pluralist political and intellectual culture, it was striking that in the 1950s West Germans remained largely fixated on the losses Germans had borne in the war, while refusing to confront responsibility for Nazi crimes. This was not incompatible with governmental acts of restitution to Jewish survivors and the state of Israel which were not paralleled in the DDR. But in neither Germany were many of the guilty ever brought to justice, nor was victim status conferred on unpopular minorities persecuted by the Nazis, such as 'Gypsies' and homosexual men.

Only with the generational shifts of the 1960s and growing demands for real rather than formal democratization was there a perceptible move among some West Germans to confront the deeper history and consequences of National Socialism, and to reappraise what it meant to be German. Recognition of the deficit of public debate about Nazism was also prompted by the publicity surrounding a series of important new trials: the trial of ten members of Einsatzgruppe A in Ulm in 1958; the bringing to justice of Adolf Eichmann in Jerusalem in 1961; and the trial of twenty Auschwitz perpetrators in Frankfurt beginning in December 1963. These lengthy trials not only brought immense quantities of new evidence directly into the public eye but also presented fresh insights into the scope of Nazi criminality—from the mass murderers in Auschwitz and the killing fields to the 'desk murderers' who organized and facilitated their actions.

Trials left the majority of the guilty unscathed, and were only one way of appraising responsibility. The broader shifts in political and historical culture that followed after the SPD joined the West German federal government in 1966 opened up new domestic and international perspectives. Historians entered the arena of public debate with provocative propositions about deeper continuities in German aggression since 1914, which challenged the comforting view of 1933–45 as an anomaly in German history. From this it was a short step to the influential argument, already mentioned in Chapter 2, that it was not National Socialism that was abnormal, but, more disturbingly, the history of modern Germany itself—a nation exposed to political deformation by its faltering history of modernization. Whether National Socialism had furthered or hindered this process was vigorously disputed among scholars, but a greater issue for politicians and the public was the practical meaning of 'coming to terms with', 'working through', or 'mastering' the Nazi past. Was this, as liberals and social democrats insisted, not a one-off bout of enlightenment or act of catharsis but a permanent political and ethical obligation placed on the German people, an integral part of Germany's national identity for the foreseeable future? Or had the time now come, as conservatives contended, for Germany's history and identity to be unshackled from this one atypical episode, so that the Germans could recover a continuous and 'usable' sense of their historic identity on the same basis as any other nation? And what contexts of historical comparison were appropriate that did not run the risk of relativizing or belittling the full criminality of the Nazi regime?

The fall of the Berlin Wall and the unification of Germany in 1989/90 unexpectedly displaced these debates about German identity. Whatever the domestic political repercussions of unification, its peaceful achievement and aftermath reassured

Germany's neighbours that this was not the first step to a resurgent German nationalism. Since then, the accelerating accumulation of new historical research—the work not only of scholars but of citizens' groups uncovering the evidence of Nazi criminality on their own doorsteps—thrust the enormity of the Nazi regime into the West German public eye afresh. It also increasingly highlighted the centrality of antisemitism to the entire Nazi project, and it showed that shared condemnation of National Socialism did not preclude intense and fruitful controversies about the character of the regime and its legacy to the present.

Public understanding of National Socialism has accordingly been substantially repositioned in Germany and the wider world. At the same time as the Nazi period has become more closely and exclusively identified with the 'Holocaust' (a term rarely used before the 1970s), a culture of collective memory and memorialization has accumulated, supplementing judicial accountability and the historical record with highly visible monuments, historical sites, museums, and public commemorations. Germany's obligation to take moral responsibility for the nation's Nazi past was embedded in official acts such as the 1996 designation of 27 January, the anniversary of the liberation of Auschwitz, as an official day of commemoration of the victims of Nazism, and the inauguration of the Memorial to the Murdered Jews of Europe in the centre of Berlin in 2005.

Meanwhile, the memory of the Holocaust has also been widely internationalized: not only through its growing centrality to the national identity of Israel, but also with events such as the opening of the United States Holocaust Memorial Museum in Washington, DC, in 1993, the Declaration of the Stockholm International Forum on the Holocaust in 2000, and, in 2005, the United Nations' endorsement of 27 January as an international day of remembrance. European countries have embraced their own cultures of memorialization. These initiatives have certified the designation of the Holocaust as a challenge to all humanity, thereby distributing some of Germany's own burden of moral obligation to the entire world. They responded to other pressures, too: belated confrontations with national histories of complicity or silence under Nazi occupation; renewed disquiet about the threat and actuality of genocide and ethnic cleansing in Europe and the world since the late 20th century; and anxieties that, with the passing of the last contemporaries of the Nazi era, its lessons would begin to fade.

Yet the search for the interpretation and understanding of National Socialism must not be confined to the ultimate horror of the Holocaust. This event will continue to test our moral understanding and explanatory ability to the limits, but Nazi Germany confronts us with other profound questions about the resilience of democratic culture and civil society that are not peculiar to that history alone, and these are not the least of the 'lessons' of National Socialism. Nazi Germany was built on a host of threats to the values of democracy and pluralism that were not confined to the twelve brazen years of dictatorship, terror, and mass murder and that call us to constant vigilance: the siren song of demagogues, the political exploitation of popular fears and resentments, the retreat of confidence in public institutions, the structural power of economic and political elites, the corrosion of governmental standards, the weaponization of prejudice, the repression of difference and dissent, and the eternal temptation of the blind eye.

Chronology

1889

20 Apr.   Adolf Hitler born in Braunau-am-Inn, Austria

1914

Aug.   Outbreak of First World War. Hitler enlists in Bavarian army

1918

Nov.   Armistice. Kaiser abdicates. German Republic proclaimed

1919

Jan.   Communist rising in Berlin
5 Jan.   Foundation of German Workers' Party (DAP) in Munich
19 Jan.   National Assembly elected
Feb.   National Assembly convenes in Weimar to draft constitution
Apr.–May   'Soviet Republic' in Munich
28 June   Versailles Treaty signed
11 August   Weimar constitution adopted
12 Sept.   Hitler joins the DAP

1920

24 Feb.   DAP changes name to National Socialist German Workers' Party (NSDAP)

1921

29 July   Hitler made leader of NSDAP
Nov.   SA (Stormtroopers) founded

1923

11 Jan.   French troops occupy the Ruhr
Oct.   Communist risings in Saxony and Thuringia

8/9 Nov.	Hitler's failed 'beer-hall' putsch in Munich. NSDAP (and KPD) banned
1924	
1 Apr.	Hitler sentenced for treason. Composes *Mein Kampf* in prison
20 Dec.	Hitler released from prison
1925	
Feb.	NSDAP refounded; SS established
26 Apr.	Hindenburg elected president of Germany
1928	
20 May	Reichstag elections: NSDAP wins 2.6 per cent of vote (12 seats)
1929	
20 Jan.	Himmler appointed as leader (Reichsführer) of SS
4 Oct.	US stock market crash
1930	
30 Mar.	Heinrich Brüning appointed chancellor
14 Sept.	Reichstag elections: NSDAP wins 18.3 per cent of vote (107 seats)
1931	
May	German bank crisis
1932	
10 Apr.	Hindenburg re-elected as president
30 May	Papen appointed chancellor
31 July	Reichstag elections: NSDAP wins 37.3 per cent of vote (230 seats)
6 Nov.	Reichstag elections: NSDAP wins 33.1 per cent of vote (196 seats)
2 Dec.	Schleicher appointed chancellor
1933	
30 Jan.	Hitler appointed chancellor
27 Feb.	Reichstag Fire
28 Feb.	Decree for the Protection of People and State ('Reichstag Fire Decree')
5 Mar.	Reichstag elections: NSDAP wins 43.9 per cent of vote (288 seats)
9 Mar.	Himmler appointed commissar of Bavarian political police

20 Mar.	Dachau concentration camp established
21 Mar.	Special courts (Sondergerichte) established
23 Mar.	Enabling Act passed
1 Apr.	Boycott of Jewish shops
26 Apr.	Gestapo established in Prussia
2 May	Trade unions dissolved; Deutsche Arbeitsfront (DAF) founded
14 July	NSDAP declared sole legal party
14 July	Law for compulsory sterilization adopted
20 July	Concordat with Vatican
14 Oct.	Germany leaves the League of Nations and Disarmament Conference

1934

26 Jan.	Non-Aggression Pact between Germany and Poland
14 Feb.	Law for the Reconstruction of the Reich abolishes German federalism
10 Apr.	Himmler appointed Inspector of Prussian Gestapo, Heydrich as deputy
24 Apr.	'People's Court' (Volksgerichtshof) established
30 June	'Night of Long Knives' ('Röhm putsch'): murder of SA leaders and other political opponents
2 Aug.	Death of Hindenburg; Hitler given title 'Führer and Reich Chancellor' and made commander-in-chief of the armed forces
Sept.	Schacht's 'New Plan' for the economy

1935

13 Jan.	Saar votes to rejoin Germany
16 Mar.	Military conscription introduced
15 Sept.	Nuremberg Laws codifying antisemitic discrimination adopted

1936

7 Mar.	Remilitarization of the Rhineland
17 June	Himmler appointed Leader of the SS and Chief of the German Police
1 Aug.	Olympic Games open in Berlin
18 Oct.	Göring appointed head of the Four Year Plan
1 Nov.	Rome–Berlin Axis announced
25 Nov.	Anti-Comintern Pact of Germany and Japan

1937

Mar.	Mass arrests of released convicts and suspected criminals
5 Nov.	Hitler describes his plans for Germany's expansion at the 'Hossbach Conference'
27 Nov.	Schacht dismissed as minister for economic affairs.

1938

Feb.	Blomberg dismissed as war minister and Fritsch as commander of army; Hitler assumes personal command of the armed forces; Neurath replaced by Ribbentrop as foreign minister
12 Mar.	German troops march into Austria
10 Apr.	*Anschluss* approved by Austrian plebiscite
29 Sept.	Sudeten crisis resolved by Munich Agreement; Czechoslovakia partitioned
27 Oct.	Jews of Polish nationality expelled from Germany
9/10 Nov.	Organized pogrom against Jews in Germany (*Kristallnacht*)
Nov./Dec.	Extensive new antisemitic measures adopted

1939

15 Mar.	German troops occupy Bohemia and Moravia
22 May	German–Italian military alliance (Pact of Steel)
23 Aug.	Nazi–Soviet Non-Aggression Pact
1 Sept.	Germany invades Poland
3 Sept.	Britain and France declare war on Germany
27 Sept.	Creation of Reichssicherheitshauptamt
Oct.	Hitler signs 'euthanasia' order (backdated to 1 Sept.)
7 Oct.	Himmler appointed 'Reich Comissioner for the Strengthening of the German Nation'

1940

9 Apr.	Germany invades Denmark and Norway
Apr.	T-4 'euthanasia' central office established
30 Apr.	Łodz ghetto established
10 May	Germany invades Belgium, the Netherlands, Luxembourg, and France
May/June	Auschwitz established as forced labour camp for POWs
26 May–4 June	Dunkirk evacuation; German armistice with France
10 July	'Battle of Britain' begins
15 Nov.	Warsaw ghetto established

1941

6 Apr.	Germany invades Yugoslavia and Greece
May	'Hunger Plan' to engineer mass famine in the occupied Soviet Union
22 June	'Operation Barbarossa': Germany invades the Soviet Union
31 July	Göring instructs Heydrich to undertake a 'comprehensive solution of the Jewish Question'
19 Sept.	Jews in Germany required to wear yellow star badge
7 Dec.	Japanese attack on Pearl Harbor
8 Dec.	Chełmno (Kulmhof) killing centre established
11 Dec.	Germany declares war on the United States

1942

20 Jan.	Wannsee Conference to coordinate the 'Final Solution of Jewish Question' in Europe
8 Feb.	Albert Speer appointed minister for armaments and munitions
May	'Generalplan Ost' for exploitation of eastern Europe drafted
4 June	SD chief Heydrich dies after assassination by Czech resistance
Summer	'Aktion Reinhard' round-up of Polish Jews for extermination in Bełżec, Sobibór, and Treblinka
Sept.	Battle for Stalingrad begins
Nov.	German troops occupy Vichy France; British victory at El Alamein

1943

31 Jan.	German VIth army surrenders at Stalingrad
Feb.	'White Rose' resistance group in Munich broken up and leaders executed
18 Feb.	Goebbels's 'total war' speech
19 Apr.	Warsaw ghetto rising begins
10 July	Allied landings in Sicily
28 July	Allied bombing of Hamburg
Aug.	German summer offensive in Russia defeated
Sept.	Germany occupies most of Italy and Italian-occupied parts of Yugoslavia, Greece, and France

1944

Mar./Oct.	German troops occupy Hungary
6 June	Allied landings in Normandy

20 July	'July Plot' to assassinate Hitler fails
23 July	Goebbels appointed 'Plenipotentiary for Total War Mobilization'
Aug.–Oct.	Warsaw Rising of Polish Home Army
25 Sept.	*Volkssturm* militia established

1945

Jan.	Soviet troops enter German territory
13–15 Feb.	Allied bombing of Dresden
27 Jan.	Auschwitz liberated by Soviet troops
4–11 Feb.	Allies' Yalta Conference on post-war settlement
30 Apr.	Hitler commits suicide in Berlin
8 May	Unconditional surrender of Germany to Allies

References

Chapter 1: Hitler myths

O. Wagener, *Hitler: Memoirs of a Confidant*, ed. H. A. Turner (Yale University Press, 1985), p. 3. Other contemporaries: C. Schmölders, *Hitler's Face: The Biography of an Image* (University of Pennsylvania Press, 2006), pp. 150, 152. Orwell, 'Review, *Mein Kampf* by Adolf Hitler', in *The Collected Essays: Journalism and Letters of George Orwell*, ed. S. Orwell and I. Angus (Penguin, 1970), vol. 2: *My Country Right or Left*, p. 28. K. Heiden, in Schmölders, *Hitler's Face*, p. 152.

Orwell, *Collected Essays*, vol. 2, p. 29.

Berlin diarists: U. von Kardorff, *Berliner Aufzeichnungen aus den Jahren 1942-1945* (Deutscher Taschenbuch Verlag, 1964), p. 242 (2 May 1945) and Anonyma, *Eine Frau in Berlin: Tagebuch-Aufzeichnungen vom 20. April bis 22. Juni 1945* (btb-Verlag, 2005), p. 123.

Weekly World News, 21 Nov. 1989 and 18 Nov. 2003; *Daily Express*, 6 Mar. 2016.

Rudolf Hess, speech at NSDAP Nuremberg rally 1934.

Joseph Goebbels, speech 20 May 1933, in H. Heiber, ed., *Goebbels: Reden*, vol. 1: *1932-1939* (Droste, 1971), p. 110.

D. Guérin, *The Brown Plague: Travels in Late Weimar and Early Nazi Germany* (Duke University Press, 1994), pp. 98-9.

M. Weber, *The Theory of Social and Political Organization*, ed. T. Parsons (Free Press, 1964), pp. 358-9.

R. Misch, *Der letzte Zeuge: Ich war Hitlers Telefonist, Kurier und Leibwächter* (Pendo, 2008), p. 70.

Wagener, *Hitler. Memoirs of a Confidant*, p. 180.

Chapter 2: National Socialism

'first national socialist', cited in C. Schmitz-Berning, *Vokabular des Nationalsozialismus* (Walter de Gruyter, 2007), p. 419.

F. Naumann, *Demokratie und Kaisertum* (Hilfe, 1900), p. 229.

T. Weber, *Hitler's First War: Adolf Hitler, the Men of the List Regiment, and the First World War* (Oxford University Press, 2010), p. 233.

Chapter 3: From Munich to Berlin (via Weimar)

E. Jäckel, *Hitler: Sämtliche Aufzeichnungen 1905–1924* (Deutsche Verlags-Anstalt, 1980), p. 620.

G. Reuth, ed., *Joseph Goebbels: Tagebücher*, vol. 1: *1924–1929* (Piper, 1992), p. 200.

K. G. W. Ludecke, *I Knew Hitler: The Story of a Nazi who Escaped the Blood Purge* (Jarrolds, 1938), pp. 217–18.

'Berlin, die unfruchtbarste Stadt der Welt', *Völkischer Beobachter*, 30 Apr. 1929, cited in B. Miller Lane, *Architecture and Politics in Germany 1918–1945* (Harvard University Press, 1968), p. 155.

Völkischer Beobachter, 3 July 1926, cited in A. Tyrell, *Führer befiehl . . . Selbstzeugnisse aus der 'Kampfzeit' des NSDAP* (Droste, 1969), p. 156.

J. Goebbels, *Das erwachende Berlin* (Franz Eher Verlag, 1934), p. 17.

Solmitz, in W. Jochmann, ed., *Nationalsozialismus und Revolution: Ursprung und Geschichte der NSDAP in Hamburg, 1922–1933: Dokumente* (Europäischer Verlag, 1963), p. 421.

Goebbels, 31 Jan. 1933 in Reuth, ed., *Joseph Goebbels: Tagebücher*, vol. 2, p. 757.

Chapter 4: Power

Reuth, ed.*Goebbels: Tagebücher*, vol. 2, p. 785.

U. von Hassell, *Die Hassell–Tagebücher 1938–1944*, ed. Friedrich Freiherr von Gaertringen (Siedler, 1989), 1 Nov. 1939, p. 138.

'organized chaos', Leo Killy, cited in D. Rebentisch, *Führerstaat und Verwaltung im Zweiten Weltkrieg* (Franz Steiner, 1989), p. 533.

E. R. Huber, *Verfassungsrecht des Grossdeutschen Reiches*
(Hanseatische Verlag, 1939), p. 197. *Hans Schemm spricht: Hans
Schemm spricht. Sein Leben und sein Werk*, ed. G. Kahl-Furthmann
(Gauleitung der Bayrischen Ostmark, 1935), p. 242.

R. Hess, *Reden* (Franz Eher Verlag, 1938), p. 7.

'choosing not to choose': J. P. Stern, *Hitler: The Führer and the People*
(Fontana, 1975), p. 23; 'work[ed] towards the Führer': Werner
Willikens, cited in I. Kershaw, *Hitler. 1889–1936: Hubris*
(Allen Lane, 1998), p. 530.

'Organized subhumanity', cited in P. Longerich, *Heinrich Himmler*
(Oxford University Press, 2012), p. 198.

Chapter 5: *Volksgemeinschaft*: Community and exclusion

'applied biology': Hans Schemm, cited in R. N. Proctor, *Racial
Hygiene: Medicine under the Nazis* (Harvard University Press,
1988), p. 64.

Reinhardt Heydrich, 'Durchführungsrichtlinien zum Grunderlass
Vorbeugende Verbrechensbekämpfung', 4 Apr. 1938, in Wolfgang
Ayass, ed., *Materialien aus dem Bundesarchiv*, vol. 5:
*'Gemeinschaftsfremde': Quellen zur Verfolgung von 'Asozialen'
1933–1945* (Bundesarchiv Koblenz, 1998), p. 275.

Bavarian political police in M. Broszat, 'The Concentration Camps', in
H. Krausnick, H. Buchheim, M. Broszat, and H.-A. Jacobsen,
Anatomy of the SS State (Walker, 1968), p. 450.

V. Klemperer, *I Will Bear Witness 1933–1941: A Diary of the Nazi
Terror* (Random House, 1990), 9 Oct. 1938, p. 272.

K. Wünschmann, *Before Auschwitz: Jewish Prisoners in the Prewar
Concentration Camps* (Cambridge University Press, 2015), p. 201.

Chapter 6: *Volksgemeinschaft*: Control and belonging

V. Klemperer, *The Language of the Third Reich. LTI—LinguaTertii
Imperii: A Philologist's Notebook* (Continuum, 2000), chapter 30.

V. Klemperer, *Ich will Zeugnis ablegen bis zum letzten: Tagebücher
1933–1941* (Aufbau, 1995), 13 June 1934, p. 114.

Orwell, 'Funny, but not Vulgar', 28 July 1945, in Orwell, *Collected
Essays*, vol. 3: *As I Please 1943–1945*, p. 325. H.-J. Gamm, *Der
Flüsterwitz im Dritten Reich* (Paul List, 1966), pp. 62, 49.

References

Chapter 8: War

Hitler's boast in J. Noakes and G. Pridham, eds, *Nazism 1919–1945*, vol. 3: *Foreign Policy, War and Racial Extermination* (Exeter, 2001), p. 249.

Adolf Hitler to Benito Mussolini, 21 June 1942, in *Documents on German Foreign Policy 1918–1945*, Series D (1937–1955), vol. 12: *The War Years Feb. 1 – June 22, 1941*, pp. 1069, 1068.

Chapter 9: From terror to genocide

H. Lévy-Hass, *Diary of Bergen-Belsen 1944–1945*, ed. Amira Hass (Haymarket Press, 2009), p. 120.

Hitler order, backdated to 1 Sept., facsimile in H. Friedlander, *The Origins of Nazi Genocide: From Euthanasia to the Final Solution* (University of North Carolina Press, 1995), facing page title.

A. Adelson, L. Langer, and K. Turowski, eds, *The Diary of Dawid Sierakowiak: Five Notebooks from the Lodz Ghetto* (Oxford University Press, 1998), 4 Sept. 1942, p. 215.

Gauleiter Kube, 16 Dec. 1941, cited in P. Rentrop, 'Die "Sonderghettos" für deutsche Jüdinnen und Juden im besetzten Minsk (1941–1943)', in B. Meyer, ed., *Deutsche Jüdinnen und Juden in Ghettos und Lagern (1941–1945)* (Metropol, 2017), p. 101.

Hitler prophecy, M. Domarus, ed., *Hitler. Reden und Proklamationen 1932–1945*, vol. 2, Part 1, 1939–1940 (R. Löwit, 1973), p. 1058. Report of Hitler speech in *Die Tagebücher von Joseph Goebbels*, ed. E. Fröhlich, vol. 2: *Diktate 1941–1945* (Saur, 1993–6), 13 Dec. 1941, p. 498. Hans Frank speech in W. Präg and W. Jacobmeyer, eds, *Das Diensttagebuch des deutschen Generalgouverneurs in Polen 1939–1945* (Deutsche Verlags-Anstalt, 1975), p. 457.

Wannsee minutes: Besprechungsprotokoll, facsimile from Gedenkstätte Haus der Wannseekonferenz: <https://www.ghwk.de/fileadmin/user_upload/pdf-wannsee/dokumente/protokoll-januar1942_barrierefrei.pdf > (accessed May 13, 2019).

Dr Buchmann, 31 May 1942, cited at <http://jüdische-gemeinden.de/index.php/gemeinden/u-z/2053-weimar-thueringen>.

A. I. Katsh, ed., *The Warsaw Diary of Chaim A. Kaplan* (Collier, 1973), p. 144.

Buchenwald order in *Buchenwald: Mahnung und Verpflichtung. Dokumente und Berichte* (Deutscher Verlag der Wissenschaften, 1983), p. 640.

Epilogue

S. Lehnstaedt and K. Lehnstaedt, 'Fritz Sauckels Nürnberger Aufzeichnungen. Erinnerungen aus seiner Haft während des Kriegsverbrecherprozesses', *Vierteljahrshefte für Zeitgeschichte*, vol. 57/1 (2009), p. 126.

H. Arendt, 'The Aftermath of Nazi Rule: Report from Germany', *Commentary*, vol. 10 (Jan. 1950), p. 342.

'desk murderers' coined by Arendt in her preface to B. Naumann, *Auschwitz: A Report on the Proceedings against Robert Karl Ludwig Mulka and Others before the Court at Frankfurt* (Pall Mall, 1966), p. xi.

Further reading

Introductions and overviews

The best overviews of Nazi Germany are T. Childers, *The Third Reich: A History of Nazi Germany* (Simon and Schuster, 2017); the three volumes by R. J. Evans, *The Coming of the Third Reich*; *The Third Reich in Power, 1933–1939*; and *The Third Reich at War: How the Nazis Led Germany from Conquest to Disaster* (Penguin, 2004–9); and M. Burleigh, *The Third Reich: A New History* (Macmillan, 2000). I. Kershaw, *The Nazi Dictatorship: Problems and Perspectives of Interpretation* (Bloomsbury, 2015), plots the changing historiographical scene. Handbooks with comprehensive bibliographies include S. Baranowski and A. Nolzen, eds, *A Companion to Nazi Germany* (Wiley Blackwell, 2018); J. Caplan, ed., *Nazi Germany* (Oxford University Press, 2008); and P. Hayes, ed., *Oxford Handbook of Holocaust Studies* (Oxford University Press, 2010). An indispensable combination of narrative history and primary sources is J. Noakes and G. Pridham, eds, *Nazism 1919–1945: A Documentary Reader*, 4 vols. Reliable websites for primary sources in translation include:
<http://www.germanhistorydocs.ghi-dc.org/home.cfm>; <http://eudocs.lib.byu.edu/index.php/History_of_Germany%3A_Primary_Documents>
<http://www.calvin.edu/academic/cas/gpa/ww2era.htm> (accessed May 10, 2019).

Biographies

The best biography of Hitler is I. Kershaw, *Hitler, 1889–1936: Hubris*;
and *Hitler, 1836–1945: Nemesis* (Penguin, 2001); see also V. Ullrich,
Hitler, vol. 1: *Ascent 1889–1939* (Penguin Random House, 2017);
Peter Longerich, *Hitler. A Life* (Oxford University Press, 2019);
Brendan Simms, *Hitler. Only the World Was Enough* (Allen Lane,
2019). Other biographies include D. Cesarani, *Eichmann: His Life
and Crimes* (Vintage, 2005); C. Epstein, *Model Nazi: Arthur
Greiser and the Occupation of Western Poland* (Oxford University
Press, 2010); J. Fest, *The Face of the Third Reich: Portraits of the
Nazi Leadership* (I. B. Tauris, 2001); R. Gerwarth, *Hitler's
Hangman: The Life of Heydrich* (Yale University Press, 2011);
E. Hancock, *Ernst Röhm: Hitler's SA Chief of Staff* (Palgrave
Macmillan, 2011); M. Housden, *Hans Frank: Lebensraum and the
Holocaust* (Palgrave Macmillan, 2003); Peter Longerich, *Heinrich
Himmler* (Oxford University Press, 2012) and his *Goebbels: A
Biography* (Vintage, 2016); R. Overy, *Göring: Hitler's Iron Knight*
(I. B. Tauris, 2012). For lower-ranking careers, see M. Wildt, *An
Uncompromising Generation: The Nazi Leadership of the Reich
Security Main Office* (University of Wisconsin Press, 2010) and
A. J. Kay, *The Making of an SS Killer: The Life of Colonel Albert
Filbert, 1900–1990* (Cambridge University Press, 2016).

Chapter 1: Hitler myths

Sources for this chapter include D. M. McKale, *Hitler: The Survival Myth*
(Stein and Day, 1981); C. Schmölders, *Hitler's Face: The Biography of
an Image* (University of Pennsylvania Press, 2006); G. D. Rosenfeld,
*The World Hitler Never Made: Alternate History and the Memory of
Nazism* (Cambridge University Press, 2005); G. D. Rosenfeld, *Hi
Hitler! How the Nazi Past is being Normalized in Contemporary
Culture* (Cambridge University Press, 2015); I. Kershaw, *The Hitler
Myth: Image and Reality in the Third Reich* (Oxford University Press,
2001); and J. P. Stern, *Hitler: The Führer and the People* (Fontana,
1990). For debates about fascism and totalitarianism, see R. O. Paxton,
The Anatomy of Fascism (Penguin, 2005); R. J. B. Bosworth, ed., *The
Oxford Handbook of Fascism* (Oxford University Press, 2009);
B. F. Pauley, *Hitler, Stalin, and Mussolini: Totalitarianism in the
Twentieth Century* (Chichester, 2015); Kevin Passmore, *Fascism: A
Very Short Introduction* (Oxford University Press, 2002).

Chapter 2: National Socialism

B. Anderson, *Imagined Communities: Reflections on the Origin and Spread of Nationalism* (Verso, 1991) is a classic essay on nationalism and nation-building. For the political culture of imperial Germany see D. Blackbourn and G. Eley, *The Peculiarities of German History: Bourgeois Society and Politics in Nineteenth-Century German History* (Oxford University Press, 1984), and C. Applegate, *A Nation of Provincials: The German Idea of Heimat* (University of California Press, 1990). On right-wing ideologies, see G. L. Mosse, *The Crisis of German Ideology: Intellectual Origins of the Third Reich* (Weidenfeld and Nicolson, 1966); P. Pulzer, *The Rise of Political Anti-Semitism in Germany and Austria* (Harvard University Press, 1988); and C. Schorske, *Fin-de-siècle Vienna: Politics and Culture* (Cambridge University Press, 1981). R. Weikart, *From Darwin to Hitler: Evolutionary Ethics, Eugenics, and Racism in Germany* (Palgrave Macmillan, 2004) is a bold interpretation. Hitler's life before 1918 is investigated by B. Hamann, *Hitler's Vienna: A Dictator's Apprenticeship* (Tauris Parke, 2010) and T. Weber, *Hitler's First War: Adolf Hitler, the Men of the List Regiment, and the First World War* (Oxford University Press, 2010). For the ending of the war, see R. Gerwarth, *The Vanquished: Why the First World War Failed to End, 1917–1923* (Penguin, 2017).

Chapter 3: From Munich to Berlin (via Weimar)

For the three cities that frame this chapter, see D. C. Large, *Where Ghosts Walked. Munich's Road to the Third Reich* (Norton, 1997); M. Kater, *Weimar: From Enlightenment to the Present* (Yale University Press, 2014), and T. Friedrich, *Hitler's Berlin: Abused City* (Yale University Press, 2012). Hitler's path to National Socialism is discussed in T. Weber, *Becoming Hitler: The Making of a Nazi* (Oxford University Press, 2017); the history of the NSDAP in D. Orlow, *The History of the Nazi Party*, 2 vols (University of Pittsburgh Press, 1969–73), the SA in D. Siemens, *Stormtroopers: A New History of Hitler's Brownshirts* (Yale University Press, 2017) and P. H. Merkl, *The Making of a Stormtrooper* (Princeton University Press, 1980). For Weimar Germany, see E. D. Weitz, *Weimar Germany* (Princeton University Press, 2007), A. McElligott, ed., *Weimar Germany* (Oxford University Press, 2009) and D. Peukert, *The Weimar Republic. The Crisis of Classical Modernity*

(Penguin, 1993). The depression is covered in H. James, *The German Slump: Politics and Economics, 1924–1936* (Clarendon Press, 1987). For the NSDAP, see P. Madden and D. Mühlberger, *The Nazi Party: The Anatomy of a People's Party, 1919–1933* (Peter Lang, 2007); T. Childers, *The Nazi Voter: The Social Foundations of Fascism in Germany, 1919–1933* (University of North Carolina Press, 1983); and J. Sneeringer, *Winning Women's Votes: Propaganda and Politics in Weimar Germany* (University of North Carolina Press, 2002). For the popular appeal of National Socialism before 1933, see W. S. Allen's classic *The Nazi Seizure of Power: The Experience of a Single German Town, 1930–1935* (Penguin, 1989) and P. Fritzsche, *Germans into Nazis* (Harvard University Press, 1998). Autobiographical evidence is presented in T. Abel, *Why Hitler Came into Power* (Harvard University Press, 1986) and M. Mayer, *They Thought They were Free: the Germans, 1933–1945* (University of Chicago Press, 2017).

Chapter 4: Power

The Nazi political system is discussed in M. Broszat, *The Hitler State: The Foundation and Development of the Internal Structure of the Third Reich* (Longman, 1982). For the administrative, legal, and penal systems, see E. Fraenkel, *The Dual State: A Contribution to the Theory of Dictatorship* (Oxford University Press, 2017), first published in 1941; J. Caplan, *Government without Administration: State and Civil Service in Weimar and Nazi Germany* (Clarendon Press, 1988); H. W. Koch, *In the Name of the Volk: Political Justice in Hitler's Germany* (Tauris, 1989); and N. Wachsmann, *Hitler's Prisons: Legal Terror in Nazi Germany* (Yale University Press, 2004). For the concentration camps, see N. Wachsmann, *KL: A History of the Nazi Concentration Camps* (Little, Brown, 2015); Dan Stone, *Concentration Camps: A Very Short Introduction* (Oxford University Press, 2019). C. Goeschel, ed., *The Nazi Concentration Camps, 1933–1939: A Documentary History* (University of Nebraska Press, 2012); and M. T. Allen, *The Business of Genocide: The SS, Slave Labor, and the Concentration Camps* (University of North Carolina Press, 2002). On the SS, see H. Krausnick and H. Buchheim, *Anatomy of the SS State* (Collins, 1968); see also R. L. Koehl, *The Black Corps: The Structure and Power Struggles of the Nazi SS* (University of Wisconsin Press, 1983), and C. Ingrao, *Believe and Destroy: Intellectuals in the SS War Machine* (Polity, 2013).

Chapters 5 and 6: *Volksgemeinschaft*

The best introductions are D. Peukert, *Inside Nazi Germany: Conformity, Opposition and Racism in Everyday Life* (Penguin, 1993); P. Fritzsche, *Life and Death in the Third Reich* (Harvard University Press, 2008); M. Steber and B. Gotto, eds, *Visions of Community in Nazi Germany: Social Engineering and Private Lives* (Oxford University Press, 2014); and L. Pine, *Hitler's 'National Community': Society and Culture in Nazi Germany* (Routledge, 2017). G. Aly, *Hitler's Beneficiaries: How the Nazis Bought the German People* (Verso, 2007) is a provocative outlier. V. Klemperer, *The Klemperer Diaries, 1933–1945* (Phoenix, 2000) is an indispensable source; and see his *The Language of the Third Reich: LTI—Lingua Tertii Imperii: A Philologist's Notebook* (Bloomsbury, 2013). Other studies include A. Bergerson, *Ordinary Germans in Extraordinary Times: The Nazi Revolution in Hildesheim* (Indiana University Press, 2004); S. Baranowski, *'Strength through Joy': Consumerism and Mass Tourism in the Third Reich* (Cambridge University Press, 2004); I. Guenther, *Nazi Chic? Fashioning Women in the Third Reich* (Berg, 2004); T. Mason, *Social Policy in the Third Reich: The Working Class and the 'National Community'* (Berg, 1993); and P. Swett, *Selling under the Swastika: Advertising and Commercial Culture in Nazi Germany* (Stanford University Press, 2014). On women and the family, see J. Stephenson, *Women in Nazi Germany* (Longman, 2001), L. Pine, *Nazi Family Policy, 1933–1945* (Berg, 1997), and M. Mouton, *From Nurturing the Nation to Purifying the Volk: Weimar and Nazi Family Policy, 1918–1945* (Cambridge University Press, 2007). For the history of Jewish Germans after 1933, see S. Friedländer, *Nazi Germany and the Jews: The Years of Persecution, 1933–1939* (Phoenix, 2014); and Marion Kaplan, *Between Dignity and Despair: Jewish Life in Nazi Germany* (Oxford University Press, 1998). On the relation between coercion and consent, see R. Gellately, *The Gestapo and German Society: Enforcing Racial Policy* (Clarendon Press, 1990) and his *Backing Hitler: Consent and Coercion in Nazi Germany* (Oxford University Press, 2002); E. A. Johnson, *Nazi Terror: The Gestapo, Jews, and Ordinary Germans* (John Murray, 2000); and M. Wildt, *Hitler's Volksgemeinschaft and the Dynamics of Racial Exclusion: Violence against Jews in Provincial Germany, 1919–1939* (Berghahn, 2012). For other victims of Nazi persecution, see M. Burleigh and

W. Wippermann, *The Racial State: Germany, 1933–1945*
(Cambridge University Press, 1991); M. Burleigh, *Death and
Deliverance: 'Euthanasia' in Germany c.1900–1945* (Pan, 2002);
R. Proctor, *Racial Hygiene: Medicine under the Nazis* (Harvard
University Press, 1988); G. Grau, *Hidden Holocaust? Gay and
Lesbian Persecution in Germany, 1933–1945* (Cassell, 1995);
C. Schoppmann, *Days of Masquerade: Life Stories of Lesbians
during the Third Reich* (Columbia University Press, 1996); and
G. Lewy, *The Nazi Persecution of the Gypsies* (Oxford University
Press, 2000).

Chapter 7: Preparing for war

The economics of rearmament are examined in R. Overy, *War and
Economy in the Third Reich* (Clarendon Press, 1994) and A. Tooze,
*The Wages of Destruction. The Making and Breaking of the Nazi
Economy* (Allen Lane, 2006); military perspectives in W. Deist,
The Wehrmacht and German Rearmament (Macmillan, 1981); and
big business in P. Hayes, *Industry and Ideology. IG Farben in the
Nazi Era* (Cambridge University Press, 2001). Hitler's strategic
thinking is the subject of an influential essay by E. Jäckel, *Hitler's
Weltanschauung: A Blueprint for Power* (Wesleyan University
Press, 1972); foreign policy is examined in G. L. Weinberg, *Hitler's
Foreign Policy: The Road to World War II, 1933–1939* (Enigma,
2005) and C. Leitz, *Nazi Foreign Policy, 1933–1941* (Routledge,
2004). For the 1940/1 military campaigns, see A. Rossino, *Hitler
Strikes Poland: Blitzkrieg, Ideology, and Atrocity* (University Press
of Kansas, 2003); E. R. May, *Strange Victory: Hitler's Conquest of
France* (I. B. Tauris, 2009); and, R. J Overy, *The Battle of Britain:
Myth and Reality* (Penguin, 2010).

Chapter 8: War

For Nazi Germany at war, see R. Bessel, *Nazism and War* (Weidenfeld
& Nicolson, 2004) and his *Germany 1945: From War to Peace*
(Simon & Schuster, 2009). A comprehensive history is
G. Weinberg, *A World at Arms: A Global History of World War II*
(Cambridge University Press, 2005). The war in the USSR is
covered in C. Hartmann, *Operation Barbarossa: Nazi Germany's
War in the East, 1941–1945* (Oxford University Press, 2013);

O. Bartov, *The Eastern Front, 1941–1945: German Troops and the Barbarisation of Warfare* (Palgrave, 2001); see also W. Wette, *The Wehrmacht: History, Myth, Reality* (Harvard University Press, 2006), and T. Kühne, *The Rise and Fall of Comradeship: Hitler's Soldiers, Male Bonding and Mass Violence in the Twentieth Century* (Cambridge University Press, 2017). For occupied Europe, see P. Fritzsche, *An Iron Wind: Europe under Hitler* (Basic Books, 2016) and M. Mazower, *Hitler's Empire: Nazi Rule in Occupied Europe* (Allen Lane, 2008); for Poland, M. Winstone, *The Dark Heart of Hitler's Europe: Nazi Rule in Poland under the General Government* (I. B. Tauris, 2013) and E. Harvey, *Women and the Nazi East: Agents and Witnesses of Germanization* (Yale University Press, 2003). For the bombing war, see R. Overy, *The Bombing War: Europe, 1939–1945* (Allen Lane, 2013), and D. Süss, *Death From the Skies: How the British and Germans Survived Bombing in World War II* (Oxford University Press, 2014); for the home front, N. Stargardt, *The German War: A Nation under Arms, 1939–1945* (Vintage, 2016); T. Brodie, *German Catholicism at War, 1939–1945* (Oxford University Press, 2018); J. Stephenson, *Hitler's Home Front: Württemberg under the Nazis* (Continuum, 2006); U. Herbert, *Hitler's Foreign Workers: Enforced Foreign Labour in Germany under the Third Reich* (Cambridge University Press, 1997); and I. Kershaw, *The End: Germany 1944–1945* (Penguin, 2012).

Chapter 9: From terror to genocide

D. Bergen, *War and Genocide: A Concise History of the Holocaust* (Rowman & Littlefield, 2016) is an excellent introduction. Longer studies include D. Cesarani, *Final Solution: The Fate of the Jews, 1933–1949* (Pan Books, 2017); S. Friedländer, *The Years of Extermination: Nazi Germany and the Jews, 1939–1945* (Phoenix, 2014); R. Hilberg, *The Destruction of European Jews*, 3 vols (Yale University Press, 2003); and P. Longerich, *Holocaust: The Nazi Persecution and Murder of the Jews* (Oxford, 2010). For other aspects discussed in this chapter, see J. Herf, *The Jewish Enemy: Nazi Propaganda during World War II and the Holocaust* (Harvard University Press, 2006); H. Friedlander, *The Origins of Nazi Genocide: From Euthanasia to the Final Solution* (University of North Carolina Press, 1995); C. Browning, *Ordinary Men. Reserve Police Battalion 101 and the Final Solution in Poland*

(Penguin, 2011); M. Roseman, *The Villa, the Lake, the Meeting: Wannsee and the Final Solution* (Penguin, 2003); G. J. Horwitz, *Ghettostadt: Łodz and the Making of a Nazi City* (Harvard University Press, 2008); and Gustavo Corni, *Hitler's Ghettos: Voices from a Beleaguered Society 1939–1944* (Oxford University Press, 2003). E. Johnson and K.-H. Reuband, *What We Knew: Terror, Mass Murder, and Everyday Life in Nazi Germany. An Oral History* (John Murray, 2005) is a compilation of interviews; for perpetrator testimony, see E. Klee, W. Dressen, and V. Riess, eds, *The Good Old Days: The Holocaust as Seen by its Perpetrators and Bystanders* (Konecky & Konecky, 1991). From the enormous literature by survivors, see above all P. Levi, *If This is a Man* (Abacus, 2013); C. Delbo, *Auschwitz and After* (Yale University Press, 1995); and O. D. Kulka, *Landscapes of the Metropolis of Death. Reflections on Memory and Imagination* (Penguin, 2013).

Epilogue

On German post-war experiences, see N. Gregor, *Haunted City: Nuremberg and the Nazi Past* (Yale University Press, 2008); R. G. Moeller, *War Stories: The Search for a Usable Past in the Federal Republic of Germany* (University of California Press, 2001); B. Niven, ed., *Germans as Victims: Remembering the Past in Contemporary Germany* (Palgrave Macmillan, 2006), and K. H. Jarausch, *After Hitler: Recivilizing Germans, 1945–1995* (Oxford University Press, 2006). For memory and commemoration, see M. Fulbrook, *German National Identity after the Holocaust* (Polity, 1999) and her *Reckonings: Legacies of Nazi Persecution and the Quest for Justice* (Oxford University Press, 2018); R. Koshar, *From Monuments to Traces: Artifacts of German Memory, 1870–1990* (University of California Press, 2000); and J. Herf, *Divided Memory: The Nazi Past in the Two Germanys* (Harvard University Press, 1997). D. Bloxham, *The Final Solution: A Genocide* (Oxford University Press, 2009), discusses the Holocaust in the context of other genocides.

Index

SOCIAL MEDIA
Very Short Introduction

Join our community

www.oup.com/vsi

- Join us online at the official Very Short Introductions **Facebook** page.
- Access the thoughts and musings of our authors with our online **blog**.
- Sign up for our monthly **e-newsletter** to receive information on all new titles publishing that month.
- Browse the full range of Very Short Introductions online.
- Read **extracts** from the Introductions for free.
- If you are a teacher or lecturer you can order inspection copies quickly and simply via our website.

THE SOVIET UNION
A Very Short Introduction
Stephen Lovell

Almost twenty years after the Soviet Unions' end, what are we to make of its existence? Was it a heroic experiment, an unmitigated disaster, or a viable if flawed response to the modern world? Taking a fresh approach to the study of the Soviet Union, this Very Short Introduction blends political history with an investigation into the society and culture at the time. Stephen Lovell examines aspects of patriotism, political violence, poverty, and ideology; and provides answers to some of the big questions about the Soviet experience.

www.oup.com/vsi